I AM NOT A TERRIBLE TWO !

DEBORAH COHEN-TENOUDJI

© 2024 Déborah COHEN-TENOUDJI

(Writing and design)

Illustrations : Fabienne Orelien « QueenMama »

Translated from French by Melanie Cosnard

All rights reserved, including the right to reproduce, edit or translate this book or portions thereof in any form whatsoever.

ISBN : 9798326184382

This book is dedicated to my children Eleha, Michael, Avi.
The initials of your names in Hebrew put together form the word « Ima », Mum.
I believe this coincidence is because you gave a dimension to my life as a mum that I would never had expected.
May the path of your lives always be filled with joy, purity and light, just like what I receive from you three everyday.

I've always had a dream : being able to reunite my three children at the age of two ! This became possible through the talent of my illustrator QueenMama

If you like the book, bring it to life!

Talk about it, offer it as a gift...

Please leave a comment on Amazon !

Thank you !

TABLE OF CONTENTS

FOREWORD

ARE TWO-YEAR-OLDS REALLY "TERRIBLE"?	13
1. GETTING TO KNOW OUR WONDERFUL TWOS	23
Key Characteristics	*23*
Navigating parenthood in the modern world	*29*
Approaching the parent-child relationship	*37*
Embracing observation in parenting	*41*
Setting verbal boundaries	*45*
2. UNLOCKING OUR CHILD'S POTENTIAL	51
Understanding intelligence	*51*
Language development	*57*
Fostering independence	*67*
Sensory exploration	*75*
Teaching self-management	*79*
Teaching the concept of time	*85*
What equipment to buy for our child?	*91*
Preferred toys	*97*
3. MANAGING THE ENVIRONMENT, NOT THE CHILD	105
Setting boundaries for reassurance	*105*
How to speak to our Wonderful Two?	*117*
Avoiding tantrums and managing emotions	*123*
Our role during a tantrum	*131*
4. ANTICIPATING CHALLENGING TIMES	141
Goodnight, little ones!	*141*
Stopping diaper use	*155*
Removing the pacifier	*167*
When mealtime becomes a challenge	*175*
Navigating screen time for little ones	*185*
TO CONCLUDE	193

FOREWORD

« I'd like to challenge a term that's weighed heavy on my heart as a mom for too long. There are two words that seem to cast a shadow because our little one is nearing two years old that's been ominously dubbed the "Terrible Two"...

The "Terrible Two" describes this supposedly difficult phase, filled with tantrums:

"Oh, it's normal, he's two, it's the age for tantrums.",

"He's constantly saying no!",

"Be careful, he's testing you!", and other similar myths...

As if these challenging behaviors don't happen at other ages. The "Terrible Two" label gets slapped on a child who melts down because a remote control was taken away, the one they found on the couch and were delightedly using to make the red light flicker.

But the decision by mom and dad that it was too delicate to play with raises the question:

"So why was it left within my reach? How can I not explore my surroundings, which to me, are as enticing as a toy store?"

Maybe it's because mom and dad have been led to believe that you're a little troublemaker, and so they've resolved not to be outwitted by a child of barely two years?

Indeed, looking after a child at this age can be exhausting, and it's easy to feel overwhelmed by their boundless energy. At times, you might feel like throwing in the towel, especially when communication proves difficult...

Yet, I think it's essential to take a step back: yes, a child from eighteen months to roughly two and a half years is full of energy, curiosity, sensitivity, and clumsiness... And naturally so, as their zest is directed towards one thing only: Life!

This little whirlwind shakes up our need for peace, cleanliness, and adult perfection. It's utterly disorienting!

But if we pause to watch this fascinating little being as they evolve from a baby into a toddler, we're bound to be mesmerized by their intelligence and their profound connection to the world around them. Their brain is constantly at work, crafting countless combinations, understanding cause and effect, absorbing new words for their "for later" bank, and adjusting to new environments...

What we might mistake for tantrums or stubbornness are actually expressions of their deepest frustrations: the injustice of wanting to engage with everything, yet having such limited control over their actions and opportunities.

This perpetual wonder is what I've come to call the **"Wonderful Two."**

(I registered "Wonderful Two®" as a trademark in 2022.)

Having the privilege to closely observe each of my three children during their "Wonderful Two's" phase has been incredibly joyful and grounding, reconnecting me with the here and now—a state that we, as adults, often struggle to maintain.

Each day brought the curiosity of what the next moment would unfold. In a world where we're already planning our next vacation, isn't there something profoundly mature about letting ourselves be captivated by the next ladybug that catches our child's eye or the next dog bark that signals a familiar presence?

If you're up for the experiment, try observing your Wonderful for twenty minutes without interruption, not restricting them in any way, but instead trying to understand what captures their interest in that moment.

Let's ditch the labels and wholeheartedly embrace this tiny individual who, if we truly listen, will guide us down the most extraordinary path!»

Back in October 2020, on my third child's second birthday, I wrote the words you've just read. That moment solidified for me that this age is more about marvel than opposition, a sentiment I'd previously experienced with my older children. This insight sparked my deep dive into understanding how to engage with children aged eighteen months to three years, eventually leading me to document my thoughts and observations in writing.

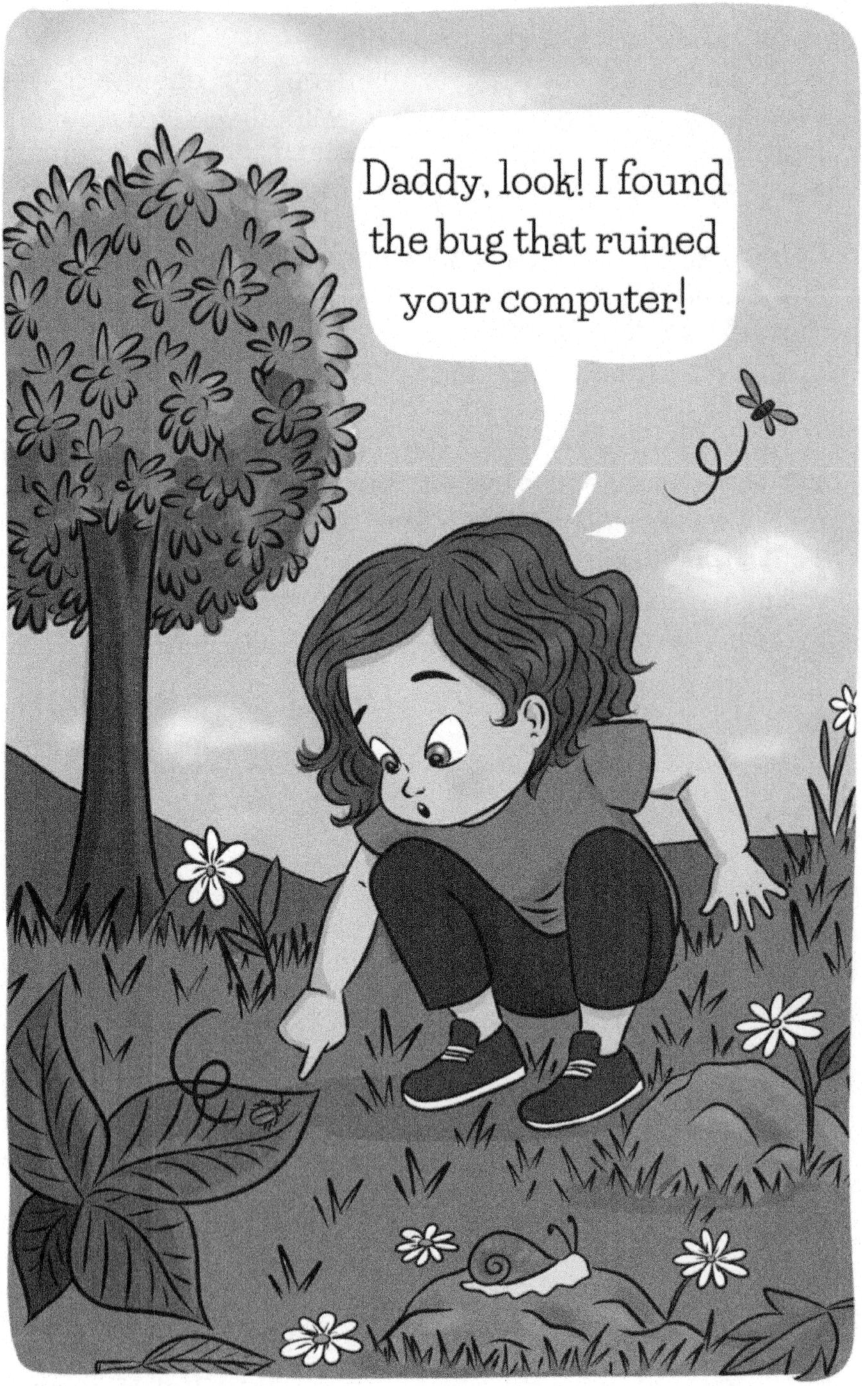
Daddy, look! I found the bug that ruined your computer!

ARE TWO-YEAR-OLDS REALLY "TERRIBLE"?

Have you ever heard of the "Terrible Two"? This popular expression describes a child's developmental phase between two and two and a half years old, suggesting that the child experiences an emotional overflow, manifesting as constant tantrums and a continual defiance against parental directives.

Depending on the context, the expression "terrible two " (with or without capital initials) both refers

1. to the period of time around two years old :

"No wonder he screams all the time, he's experiencing the terrible two!"

2. it can also work as an adjective when we used it to talk about a child.

"Kevin is a terrible two, I don't have one minute of rest!"

This phase is also referred to as the "two-year-old crisis," "the age of no," or the "oppositional phase."

This has led to a significant misunderstanding in analyzing this age, both among education professionals and the key stakeholders: parents and early childhood educators. Pinning down the exact origin of this term is challenging, but piecing together various elements can help us gain a better understanding.

In 1930, researcher Arnold Gesell conducted a study at Yale University in the United States, along with his colleagues from the Gesell Institute. His research aimed to observe the development of toddlers and was based on a small group of two-and-a-half-year-olds. Gesell concluded that the two-and-a-half-year phase is "terrible," "demonic," marking a break from what he considered the peaceful age of two.

In an article on the topic, pediatrician Dr. Heinz provides additional insight:

> The term "terrible two" was used to describe this stage and was attributed to Dr. Frances Ilg. She worked with Arnold Gesell, the renowned pediatrician and psychologist who put child development on the map. While writing my first book I called her to find out where the term came from. She laughed and said the term was a misunderstanding. The toddler's tantrum indicates normal development of the child's will as he or she becomes independent of the parent but does not yet have autonomy or know how to express feelings. Hence a meltdown. This indicates normal development and can occur earlier or later than age two.
>
> https://tucson.com/lifestyles/column/encountering-the-terrible-twos-remember-youre-in-charge/article_2a59a016-1db7-5ce5-971c-c737253e22f2.html

The misunderstanding in question revolves around two key points: firstly, the term was likely intended to be descriptive, as we can see in the 2008 document from the Gesell Institute. In this document, the Institute's members outline the characteristics of various child development stages.

For the two-and-a-half-year-old stage, among other definitions, we find:

---

2 ½ yr. Old –Break Up

- Disequilibrium
- The terrible two's
- A peak age of disequilibrium
- Rigid, Inflexible
- "No" is used often
- Cannot adapt, give in, or wait

http://mail.gesellinstitute.org/pdf/AgesAndStagesPowerPoint.pdf | Page 12

The four pages dedicated to the two-and-a-half-year-old period, although descriptive, are presented in a manner similar to this excerpt: listing only the "negative" characteristics of young children and not highlighting their skills or social, linguistic abilities, etc. The second misunderstanding is that the term "Terrible Two" was applied to around the age of two, without making a distinction for two and a half years old, even though the document is clear on this point: the "terrible" ones are the two-and-a-half-year-olds.

The phrase was later popularized in the United States and then worldwide, notably through a book... Care Bears! Yes, our beloved colorful bears, before being broadcast on television, appeared in children's books through a series of short episodes for children. In one story, little Melinda's birthday is ruined by her brother and sister, two-year-old twins, who are very excited that day.

Here are some sentences that can be found in it.

The mother : « I can't trust that terrible twosome for long ! »

The little girl : « The twins are probably going to ruin today just like they ruin every other day »

« You always spoil everything ! Now you're even trying to spoil my birthday ! »

« I think I'll run away from home. Maybe when they are three, I'll come back. »

« Dear Mom and Dad, I can't stand those terrible twos any longer, I'm leaving ! »

A Care Bear : « Two is a terrible age and twins must be twice as hard to live with. »

«They won't be two forever. »

« In a couple of months they'll have their own birthday. They won't be the terrible twos then.»

«Even though she knew the twins were still terrible, she was happy.»

The Care Bears and the Terrible Twos | 1983

Reading in video : www.youtube.com/watch?v=tBKJOqwpjEo

This particular story from the collection also played a role in spreading the notion that two-year-olds go through this "demonic" phase and turn into little tyrants. Incredible, isn't it?

In my opinion, labeling this period the "Terrible Two" is quite misleading.

The purpose of this book is precisely to show you another way to understand toddlers, free from the common stereotypes attached to this age. Clearly, I'm not denying the significant changes that occur during this stage in a young child's life. However, I'm baffled by how quickly this label, based on premature judgments, could disrupt family harmony on a global scale! Indeed, how can one assert that this phase is a normal part of child development when a child is inevitably influenced by their surrounding environment?

The conclusions I've drawn from my observations and experiences with two-year-olds form the foundation of my work. My primary subjects have been my three children, with whom I've spent considerable time and observed closely. Concurrently, I've had the opportunity to watch children up to three years old during my time in schools, childcare settings, or through the parent-child workshops I organized a few years ago.

My insights stem from my experiences, my understanding of children, my discovery of the relevance of Montessori pedagogy in education, and my intuition. I have a strong educational connection to this intuition. Surprisingly, this awareness has always been potent within me, granting me pedagogical skills and a deep understanding of children I've encountered from a young age. This strong intuition initially guided me toward teaching and then toward sharing a profound message with parents.

I believe every parent has the innate resources needed to understand their child. However, I'm aware that in today's world, it's more challenging for individuals to listen to their intuition amid an overflow of information. This book exists because I hope my advice, based on my personal journey, can shed new light and offers a different perspective on this unique period in a child's life and in the parent-child relationship.

The Terrible Two do not exist.

What does exist, however, are overwhelmed parents facing a child who was until recently a baby doing as expected, and who is trying to assert himself or herself by saying, "No."

"No, mom, dad, I'm sorry, I've grown today, I can't stay put, I have too much to discover! It's not against you, but I'm entering a new phase and I want to make the most of it!"

This marks the start of a sort of family battle between the little one yearning for more freedom and the parents unsure how to handle this burst of independence. It's understandable that this oppositional phase can be confusing, as most parents are unprepared for it. But confining our child to this "terrible" category will only heighten family tensions and create an inevitable power struggle between the parents and the developing toddler.

I want to offer another perspective, one of observation and understanding of the transformations that occur in these children from eighteen months to about three years. This approach with my own children has allowed me to enter their wonderful world of fantasy, curiosity, and desire, significantly easing our interactions, making the two-year-old phase my favorite age! This life force driving them to explore the world, understand their surroundings, and constantly interact with everything fascinates me. What I see foremost when observing a child, regardless of age, is their momentary curiosity. It's not the pen in their hand that might stain the couch. Instead, that's secondary to me: I divert their attention to something else and remove the pen without a word. Generally, this happens without any meltdowns, and I can continue to interact with them or quietly observe. They still have so many interesting things to show me!

How to read this book

My intention was for this book to be straightforward, engaging, and actionable, so I hope you find as much joy in reading it as I did in writing it. Beyond just debunking the "Terrible Two" myth, my primary aim is to equip you with ideas and actions that enrich this all-too-brief chapter in your child's development. Additionally, I aspire to guide you toward a more mindful approach to parenting.

The book is structured to offer a holistic journey through its chapters, arranged deliberately to build upon one another. That said, they're also accessible for non-linear exploration. Should you be addressing specific concerns, I recommend against cherry-picking chapters related to those issues alone, as doing so might cause you to miss the broader narrative. The scope of topics is deliberately narrowed to focus on what I deem most important to convey. For instance, I didn't cover general motor skills extensively, despite their importance in early development, opting instead to highlight themes that particularly strike a chord with me.

Remember, pedagogy isn't an exact science. This book represents a collection of my personal observations, beliefs, and lived experiences, rather than a scientific manual. Therefore, I can't promise that the strategies presented will universally apply to your child. Every parent and child is unique, and what works for one may not for another. If you encounter ideas that don't resonate, feel free to skip them. Embrace what suits you and set aside the rest. This, in my view, is the essence of tuning into our own instincts.

I've designed this book as a journey toward understanding our children better. We'll start by getting to know them from various angles. Then, we'll acknowledge that our two-year-olds are fundamentally little beings craving intellectual, sensory, and emotional fulfillment. Following that, I'll provide practical advice on managing the abundant energy that seems to burst from these tiny bodies. Lastly, we'll navigate the sometimes complex milestones leading up to the age of three.

Let's dive into this enchanting world!

Seeing it through the eyes of our Wonderful, you'll discover, changes everything!

1. GETTING TO KNOW OUR WONDERFUL TWOS

Key Characteristics

As we embark on this book, let's take a moment to outline the main characteristics of children between eighteen months and three years. It's essential to recognize that every child is unique, and no single pattern perfectly fits any age group. However, we can identify commonalities in their motor, psycho-emotional, and emotional development that provide a starting point for understanding.

From eighteen months, toddlers become more adept with their hands and bodies. They start walking and gaining confidence. They learn to use their thumb and index finger, crucial for developing fine motor skills in daily activities. This period marks the transition from babyhood to early childhood. Meanwhile, two-year-olds grapple with significant frustrations due to the gap between their strong desire to explore the world and their physical and intellectual limitations.

They wish to climb everywhere, touch everything, but they can't. They'd like to know how to open a snack package or build a tower of blocks, but they struggle. They want to play longer at a friend's house, but they can't grasp the concept of time. Thus, when it's time to leave, they experience intense frustration. They find it hard to express their desires, can't physically complete their intended actions, and don't fully understand their surroundings, leading to accumulated disappointments that often manifest as frequent tantrums, which we must learn to soothe without stifling their zest for life.

Their interest in the surrounding world

At this age, some children start speaking their first words, and generally, comprehension quickens when spoken to. Their intense interest in their surroundings can lead to cognitive overload, an excess of information that might also trigger a crisis or overflow. As we'll see, if we, as adults, minimize directives and explanations, using non-verbal cues, gestures, and looks instead, we can often ease this overload. The Wonderful Two can be overwhelmed by the pace of incoming information: sounds, sensations, parental instructions, the number of children in daycare. It's crucial to provide calm moments to balance this intense activity period.

The toddler's role in the family may shift since, though recently "the baby," our big baby starts to have different needs, changing the family dynamic. Sometimes, a new baby arrives, but our Wonderful still needs our presence just as much, possibly expressing this need through excessive behavior. It's wise to take a step back, ideally as a couple, to navigate this new stage thoughtfully.

Parental preferences

If your child shows a preference for one parent, it's likely because they find the comfort and resources they need with that parent at that moment. This preference isn't about affection but rather about the comfort that soothes them in the presence of a parent or daily caregiver. Don't take it personally; instead, observe the interactions between your child and this reassuring adult to understand why this dynamic is more comfortable for them. Often, this phase is temporary, and our child will go through various normal phases of regression and assertion.

Being observant and considering external factors that regularly impact their life allows you to adjust your behavior accordingly and address any gaps. If no external factors seem to account for a new challenging phase, time will likely resolve things on its own.

Kindness and boundaries should coexist

A toddler around two years old definitely needs clear boundaries within which they can safely explore both physically and emotionally. Contrary to popular belief, it's better to limit prohibitions to allow them exploration and self-regulation. Excessive negations, like "*NO, do NOT touch, do NOT put in your mouth, do NOT...*", only heighten aggressive behaviors.

Intellectual stimulation

The Wonderful Two is eager to learn, understand, touch, and explore. Fulfilling this thirst for knowledge is crucial for their cognitive development and language encouragement. This often-overlooked aspect can fundamentally change our relationship with our child. Many believe children don't need stimulation before starting school, limiting early learning opportunities. However, their brains are incredibly receptive before the age of six or seven.

Finding a balance is key, avoiding turning our child into a mere performer. Teaching them to think is more important than teaching them the alphabet or numbers. We'll dive deeper into this in the second part of the book.

Finally, ensuring our child gets enough sleep to recharge from their day and process all received information is essential. Their diet should match their metabolism and include playful approaches if necessary. Sleep and nutrition should not become family stressors, as they're foundational to balanced upbringing. Addressing any issues in these areas with a relaxed, pressure-free approach is always best. We'll explore this further in specific chapters.

Child development 18-36 months

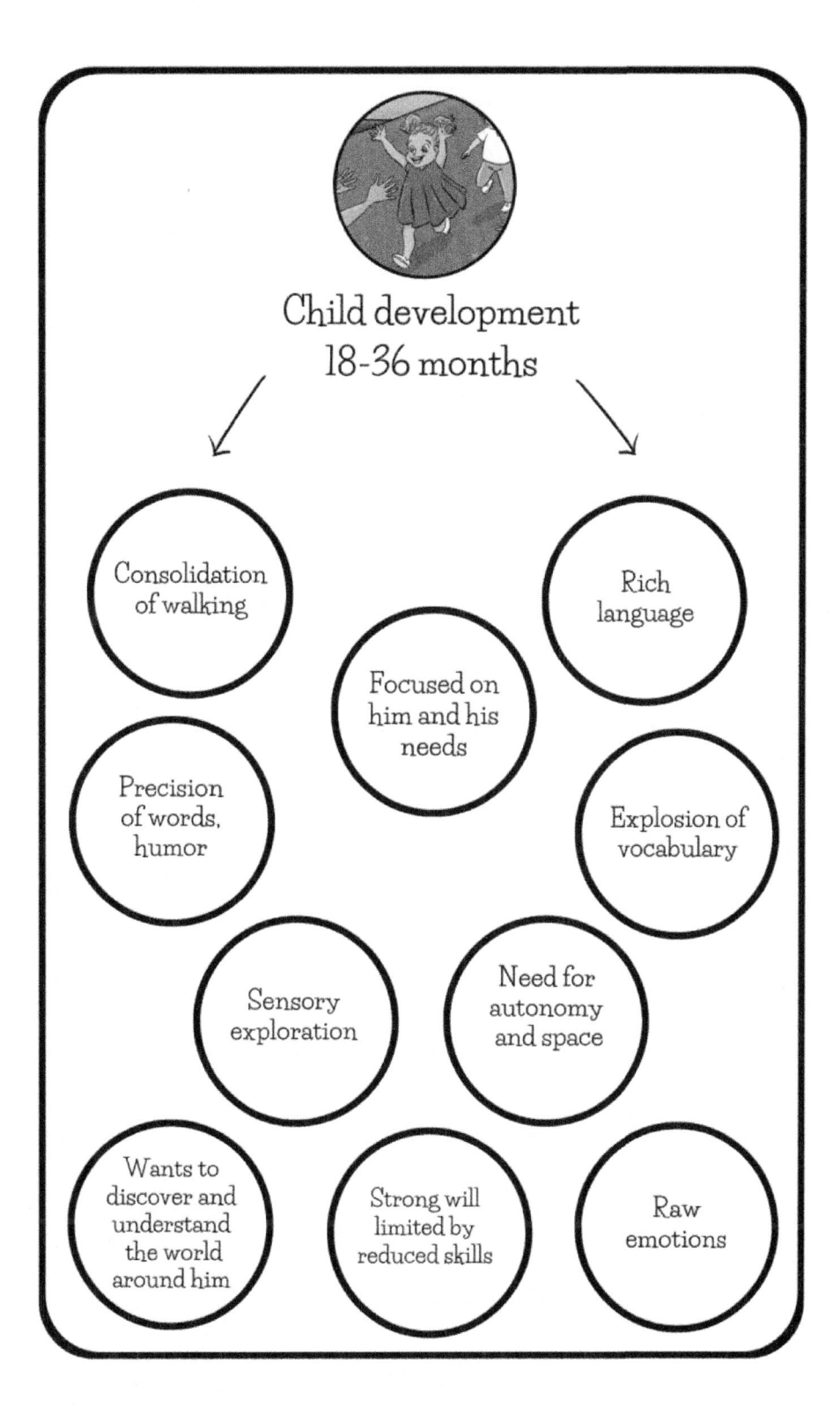

- Consolidation of walking
- Precision of words, humor
- Focused on him and his needs
- Rich language
- Explosion of vocabulary
- Sensory exploration
- Need for autonomy and space
- Wants to discover and understand the world around him
- Strong will limited by reduced skills
- Raw emotions

Navigating parenthood in the modern world

Today, it's undeniable that many parents are stretched thin, particularly due to work commitments. Nonetheless, this modern lifestyle should not detract from a young child's developmental needs. Despite the evolution of society across generations, the core needs of children remain unchanged. We can't expect our little ones to adjust to our contemporary pace of life; they're simply not equipped for it. Recognizing this, it's our responsibility to find a family balance that ensures everyone feels content and secure in their roles.

I'm deeply convinced that the intense reactions often seen in two-year-olds are largely a mirror of our own interactions with them. This observation isn't a critique of our life choices but rather an invitation to understand the complexities of this age. This stage of a child's life is energy-intensive. Children might not fully comprehend our words, expectations, or the world around them, requiring our unwavering attention and patience. Two-year-olds' behaviors, which can seem illogical to us—like biting, hitting, or causing chaos—are not always understandable to us. They demand our attention, struggle with waiting, and have yet to learn about danger or how to entertain themselves alone.

Confronted with such vitality, we often feel outmatched, despite our patience and goodwill. It's a daily challenge. We, as adults, are used to efficient, quick actions, a stark contrast to the patience required by a toddler's exploration and learning process. Adapting to this new phase is difficult; we feel a loss of the "control" we once enjoyed when our child was less mobile.

Adjusting our expectations and embracing rest

To navigate this phase with more grace, the first step is to lower our expectations of ourselves. Setting unattainable goals only adds stress to an already chaotic routine. Striving for a perpetually clean home is unrealistic with a toddler likened to a mini tornado! Lowering expectations might mean designating specific areas for play and mess or accepting that certain parts of the home will frequently be disordered. Additionally, allowing extra time for outings, preparing for potential resistance, and managing emotional outbursts can help.

By focusing on achievable tasks rather than perpetually feeling guilty for not meeting some ideal, we address the reality of our situation. We're dealing with vastly different energy levels and stages of maturity. It's natural for us not to be on the same wavelength much of the time. Hence, parents of young children need opportunities to decompress. Moving beyond the initial physical exhaustion of infancy, parenting a toddler introduces a layer of mental fatigue. Recognizing the importance of taking time for ourselves—not as a luxury, but as a necessity—is vital. We shouldn't wait until we're on the brink of a breakdown to allow ourselves a break or to seek support.

Quality time with our child

Spending quality time with our child is crucial for understanding them and deciphering their needs. Focusing entirely on them without distractions from other children, our phones, or anything else is fundamental to strengthening the parent-child bond. Our children need reassurance, and we need to adapt to their vibrant energy. These exclusive moments with them are an investment in the future of our relationship. It may seem like we don't have the time, overwhelmed with tasks, but it's through these strong connections that tranquility will gradually return. I believe that how we interact with our child during the Wonderful Two period significantly impacts our future relationship. If we can shift our perspective from viewing them as a little "terror" testing our limits to seeing them with empathy, our energy will renew even amidst challenges.

Mutual respect

Our children are highly attuned to the unspoken language of our eyes, gestures, and tone of voice, laying the groundwork for a mutual trust that serves as a pillar for our relationship going forward:

"I accept you as you are, with all your whirlwind energy and wonder. I'll do my best to guide you through this stage of your life, acknowledging my own limitations. Let's not be too hard on each other, and we'll grow together."

Just as we're forgiving of our shortcomings, we'll also extend flexibility towards our child. Their slowness, clumsiness, practical disinterest, and often incomprehensible language daily draw our attention and can trigger impulsive reactions. However, if we focus on their daily achievements, our perspective and the family atmosphere will shift for the better.

Your family is a little enterprise

One way to navigate this challenging period is to think of our child as an intern in a company. Imagine you're the boss, and this intern is here to learn their future role. Your job is to guide them through various tasks, helping them familiarize with their environment and colleagues. Of course, there are many ways to be a boss. We could be the demanding type, constantly correcting the intern for not performing up to standard, not understanding quickly enough, or making constant mistakes. As a "manager," we could find ourselves perpetually irritated and critical of our apprentice's failures. Alternatively, we could choose to be a patient and understanding boss, recognizing that our intern is in training. We accept their lack of knowledge and understand it's our responsibility to teach them, helping them excel and adapt to their new role.

Clearly, it's the latter approach we should adopt with our child, who is learning about life itself! This perspective fosters mutual respect within the small enterprise of our family. It's in a tolerant atmosphere, where we allow room for progress, that our child will feel comfortable in their environment and with their "boss." With a calm and understanding "management," they'll learn about themselves, grasp expectations, and gain confidence day by day.

Fostering kindness

By showing our child how to do things, encouraging them when it's tough, we'll make our "little intern" increasingly confident in their actions. This is how they'll feel loved and accepted at home. It's not uncommon for us to snap at our children because they're constantly by our side, knowing they won't judge our impatience or harsh words. But let's not forget these early years are pivotal for their personality development.

Of course, it's unrealistic to expect ourselves to be patient and understanding every minute, but we should strive to create an environment where our child can thrive peacefully. We need to convey that we're delighted by their presence, not annoyed by their curiosity and eagerness to explore. The magic lies in deciding to step back, not giving into the impulse to scold, even when we feel justified in our frustration. This approach not only enriches our relationship with our child but also significantly reduces tension.

Becoming an "active" parent

Unlike a "passive" parent, who often succumbs to their impulses with little consideration for their child's feelings, an "active" parent understands that their mindset significantly affects their relationship with their child and the overall household atmosphere. An active parent accepts their child as they are, cherishing the endearing aspects of their age while also acknowledging the challenges that come with parenting. By taking an active role in our parenting, reflecting, and practicing restraint, we foster a more mature relationship. This approach greatly aids in imparting our cherished values within our home and maintaining sustainable harmony.

You may already know that children absorb the general atmosphere of their home. If a child is raised in an environment filled with yelling, anger, constant prohibitions, and directives, they're more likely to emulate these behaviors. Such an atmosphere can potentially impact their psycho-emotional and even brain development. Conversely, if the home environment is generally positive, caring, and understanding, the child is empowered to fully realize their potential, even if there are occasional lapses from the parents. Their brain connections will be "programmed" to act normally, without extremes.

The Wonderful Two is merely a phase

To conclude and to offer reassurance, remember that this "stormy period" doesn't last forever. Around the age of three, or often after the first few months of preschool, children typically become more settled, calmer, and more assured in their movements. They gain greater control over their bodies, both in terms of fine and gross motor skills, and they start using words more effectively to communicate, leading to a noticeable decrease in turmoil.

But, it's important to recognize that this is just one of many challenging phases that will emerge throughout a child's life! That's why embracing these stages as they arise and striving to see the positive and beautiful aspects of our child offers a valuable approach for the long haul. The enchanting two-year-old phase is fleeting, so I urge you to make the most of these moments in the most wonderful way possible! Their small blunders are just a part of their natural development. Let's fully enjoy their smiles, their adorable attempts at words, and cherish these times as much as possible!

Daddy, could we stick my paintings on the wall like at the amusezeum?

Approaching the parent-child relationship

Some parents perceive the parent-child relationship as "vertical," placing the parent morally above the child as the keeper of knowledge. Without nuance, this relationship can become inherently unbalanced. While it's true that as adults, we possess experience and understand what's best for our child, including potential dangers and the necessity of setting healthy boundaries, this doesn't preclude treating them as complete individuals and establishing a different type of rapport.

Before becoming a mother, my experience as a first-grade teacher in a class with a small number of students taught me the value of a balanced relationship. That year, I felt that the children contributed as much to my life as I did to theirs, creating a rich classroom dynamic. The small class size allowed me to give my best without being overwhelmed by discipline. For the first time in my teaching career, I was open to learning from my students, a contrast to previous conditions that were less conducive to this reciprocal teaching method. This example parallels our role as parents, highlighting our power to define our child's place within the family, often a matter of mindset.

The limits of a "vertical" relationship

The mutual respect I experienced with my students that year is something I've strived to recreate with my children, albeit on a different emotional level. Establishing a "horizontal" relationship with our children, acknowledging our unique personalities from a young age, doesn't conflict with setting household boundaries and maintaining parental control. Our children have much to share with us, provided we listen. The foundation of the parent-child relationship is laid early and influences our child's life profoundly.

By nurturing this relationship with mutual trust and respect, our children will know they can always find support and understanding with us, through difficult times and significant milestones alike.

Honesty with our children

To foster trust, it's crucial not to lie to our children, even when they're as young as two and we think they won't remember our words shortly after. For instance, when leaving our child at daycare, we shouldn't say we'll be back in five minutes if it's not true. Our child needs to rely on our word for their emotional security. Similarly, we shouldn't use deceit to manage separations, like saying we're just fetching something from the car when we're actually leaving.

Such actions risk our child doubting our word next time or feeling insecure. Emotional security is a cornerstone of education from any age.

Instead, if we explain that we're leaving for the day, acknowledge their feelings, and express confidence in the caregivers, we set a confident tone; our child will sense this and settle more quickly. If it's hard to leave, rather than lying, we might say:

"I see you're sad I'm leaving, and I feel a bit sad too, but I know everything will be okay. Would you like to keep something of mine with you?"

Another technique I've found effective during separations is letting our child decide when we can leave:

"Let me know when it's okay for me to go, alright?"

This simple phrase empowers the child, allowing them to manage the situation and decide when they're ready for us to leave. Initially, they might take longer than we'd like, but over time, they'll remember they're in control and find reassurance in that. Children enjoy feeling in charge, and they'll likely exercise this power within a few minutes.

Embracing observation in parenting

Are you familiar with Maria Montessori? An Italian educator from the twentieth century, her name has become increasingly recognized in recent years through the widespread adoption of her educational philosophy. Discovering her journey and contributions, I was captivated by her profound understanding of children's essence, the materials she developed, and especially her educational strategies. Early in her work, especially with children with disabilities, she spent countless hours observing them to gain a deeper understanding of their behaviors and, possibly, unlock the mysteries of their personalities.

I believe this observation phase is crucial during the Wonderful Two and every significant stage of our child's life. Observing our child without interacting directly can offer numerous insights and a fresh perspective, aiding in our understanding of them. By stepping back and simply watching them without interruption, without attempting to communicate or direct their actions, we can tap into their unique world.

The greatest show on earth!

Taking the time to comfortably sit and watch our Wonderful Two navigate their world for about twenty minutes can be enlightening. This exercise will likely reveal our child's seemingly disorganized approach to exploration. Yet, we'll see their day as a series of small goals that, cumulatively, satisfy their curiosity. Suddenly, they might be drawn to explore a specific area or engage with an object, only to lose interest and move on to a new discovery. Imagine a camera mounted on their room's ceiling, capturing their day's activities in fast-forward. The energy, the dynamism, and yet, from an adult's perspective, such a whirlwind of activity can seem utterly baffling!

The present moment is all that matters

A two-year-old's curiosity knows no bounds, and our challenge is to channel it slightly while striving to preserve it. Our observations will also show that our child needs space and freedom to move, to fall, to make mistakes, and to explore freely. If they still feel the need to taste everything, let them, as long as it's safe! This can be a tough exercise for us, accustomed to curtailing actions we perceive as risky. The following chapters will detail strategies for navigating this. Our little Wonderful lives in the now, not fully recalling yesterday's events or understanding the consequences of their actions—they act for the sheer joy of the moment.

After observing, consider jotting down your thoughts and sharing them with others, as what applies to our child might not hold for another of the same age. This exercise highlights our child's uniqueness, helping us approach this tumultuous period with empathy. Understanding their lack of control can be as frustrating for them as it is for us. Focusing on the life lessons our child offers might inspire us to embrace the present, explore the world together, grow, and marvel at the simple joys life presents!

Raising children without fear

"Watch out, you might fall!"

This phrase echoes frequently from parents to their toddlers, spurred by the knowledge that their little one's coordination is still a work in progress. As they venture onto playground slides or toddle over uneven surfaces, our parental instinct kicks in, fearing a fall. Yet, shielding our children from these experiences inhibits their full engagement with the adventurous moments they seek. Often, we're looking to prevent minor mishaps that, when they do occur away from our watchful eyes, children bounce back from surprisingly fast. While it's our duty to ensure their physical safety, constant vigilance and anticipating the worst isn't necessary.

Education without fear encourages our children to develop self-reliance and mastery over their actions. They learn that falls are part of life—sometimes painful, but always surmountable. They don't constantly need us hovering for reassurance, understanding instead that actions have consequences. Through repetition, they'll navigate their way, building a crucial sense of self-confidence that benefits them for life.

Patience with developmental milestones

Furthermore, adopting a fear-free approach means resisting the urge to consult a specialist every time we suspect a developmental delay. It's natural to compare our child with peers, worrying over perceived lags in speech or motor skills. However, immediate concern is often unwarranted. This isn't to doubt the expertise of childhood development professionals, but to recognize that hastily seeking a label can sometimes uncover issues that might not be significant.

In an era quick to diagnose, discernment is key. I've encountered parents advised to seek speech therapy for an 18-month-old not yet speaking, a recommendation I find premature. Professional advice carries weight, but it's essential to differentiate between showcasing expertise and providing necessary guidance. Such situations can leave parents feeling powerless, prematurely labeling a child who might just need a bit more time.

As parents, distinguishing between identifying a genuine concern and understanding our child's unique developmental timeline is crucial. My message encourages you to trust your intuition, to listen to the inner voice that often knows best. In many cases, the insights we seek about our child's growth and needs lie within us, ready to be discovered.

Setting verbal boundaries

When upset by our child's misbehavior, whether it's hitting, drawing on the wall, or something else, we might find ourselves uttering phrases like:

"You're not being nice!
You're being naughty!
Good children don't do that!
Look at how well-behaved that little boy over there is, he listens to his parents! "

Such statements can be problematic because they directly label the child as the problem without distancing the action from the child's character. Our child isn't inherently bad; it's their action that we find inappropriate. Instead of using hurtful phrases, saying something like "It's not okay to do that; you shouldn't do that," helps separate the child from the action. This distinction is crucial as it doesn't impact their self-esteem; they won't see themselves as "naughty" but understand that certain behaviors should be avoided in the future. It's important to remember that we are our children's main role models, and seemingly innocuous remarks can significantly affect their self-worth.

Punishments, spanking, and harmful words

There will be moments when we feel overwhelmed by our Wonderful Two and eagerly await the end of this challenging phase. However, there's never justification for physical punishment, harsh words, insults, or locking them away, even if advised by a child psychologist. The inclination towards punishment is more about our own ingrained habits than about evidence-based practices. Professionals who recommend punishment, especially at this tender age, likely lack a deep understanding of its impacts. Under no circumstances should physical violence or verbal abuse be deemed acceptable. Such actions leave lasting scars, affecting the child's emotional well-being and potentially damaging the trust and bond between parent and child.

To those who argue that a spanking has never killed anyone, we must question what has been lost in their empathy to hold such a view. Our children are defenseless and look to us for protection. How can we become the source of their fear under the guise of "correction"? Resorting to physical dominance is not only damaging but undermines the very foundation of trust. Psychological trauma and the risk of eroding the parent-child relationship carry far greater consequences than many realize. No study has shown positive outcomes from physical discipline.

If you're reading this book, you're likely seeking a more conscious approach to parenting, one that doesn't include physical or verbal aggression. Despite personal challenges or upbringing, you may occasionally feel a surge of anger, as all parents do. In such moments, it's crucial to step back and pass caregiving duties to another trusted adult or caregiver. Periodically entrusting your child to a daycare or family member can provide immediate relief from physical and psychological exhaustion. Everyone is entitled to strong emotions, but no one has the right to act violently towards a child. For some parents, this may mean reevaluating deeply held beliefs. Remember, an educational approach that excludes physical and verbal violence is always preferable.

Mastering our emotions in parenting

Throughout this book, we emphasize the importance of acknowledging our child's needs and allowing them the space to grow. Yet, paramount to this is our ability to manage our own adult feelings and emotions. This often presents a challenge since many of us haven't been taught how to effectively process our emotions, neither as children nor as adults.

However, here are some straightforward strategies for calming ourselves:

- Strive to understand our own emotional processes.
- Accept that emotions ebb and flow.
- Learn to identify and understand the causes of our emotions.
- Take five-minute breaks when we feel overwhelmed.
- Recognize intense emotions before interacting with our child and not project them directly.

Nowadays, we have access to a wealth of resources on managing emotions, from books and online content to professional advice. Handling our emotions is crucial in guiding our Wonderful Two's emotional development.

Children do not make whims

Understanding, accepting, and controlling our own emotions—such as not allowing anger to dominate—reveals that our child is not merely a receptacle for our frustrations but rather a companion in life. This underscores the importance of striving to comprehend the reasons behind their tears, as there is invariably a cause, typically tied to an unmanaged emotion. We should endeavor to grasp what currently piques their interest, what they are attempting to communicate. By trusting what our children express, we validate their feelings and experiences.

These behaviors aren't "whims", "tantrums" or "fits" intended to annoy us; they are, instead, signals that convey the discomfort they are experiencing at that moment. Tears, outbursts of anger, and shouts of joy are all ways our children reach out to us, albeit awkwardly, as if saying:

"I can't articulate my feelings in words, but I need your help to find calmness. I seek a connection with you because what I'm feeling is overwhelming! I'm too young to manage this on my own! Please, find a way to help me, even if it's just a temporary fix."

It helps to parallel a toddler trying to communicate without being able to be understood with a tourist travelling in a foreign country while he cannot express himself properly. The frustration is palpable because he knows what he wants or needs but doesn't have the right words to say it. This is what our little one can feel when experiencing a situation that they can't master. Since he doesn't have the ability to control his emotions, he expresses it through anger.

Our children will trust us when we demonstrate that we are genuinely engaged with them, when we show affection and accept their whole personalities, encompassing both their laughter and joy as well as their cries of despair.

Fostering mutual trust

As previously discussed, there are numerous approaches to the parent-child relationship, each with its own set of reasons for preferring one educational strategy over another. I maintain that there is merit in every educational approach, clearly excluding any that involve humiliation or physical harm. I've observed that the more we attend to our child's needs, the stronger the trust we build with them. For instance, we face a choice when our child cries: to ignore them or leave them to deal with their emotions alone, or to engage with them, seeking to understand the root of their distress.

Such decisions, which might seem trivial, actually shape the nature of the bond between our child and us. Typically, by paying even slight attention to the reasons behind our child's emotional vulnerability, we can find ways to soothe them without compromising our authority—a concern for many parents. Embracing our little one, speaking to them, and providing distractions are immediate actions to consider before delving into deeper solutions. The section on handling meltdowns will provide more detailed tactics for navigating challenging situations, yet it's crucial to remember that our myriad small choices and actions cumulatively dictate our broader educational decisions.

A song just for you

Upon the birth of my daughter, I inexplicably felt compelled to create a song featuring her name. This song emerged spontaneously as I gazed at her, with straightforward lyrics and a simple tune, yet it became a regular means of calming her with "her" song. When her brothers were born, I followed suit, crafting a unique song for each. This practice has endured, becoming a cherished connection between me and my children, who now and then ask:

"Mom, can you sing my song, the one you wrote for me?"

This anecdote emphasizes that it's the little things that forge lasting memories and strong bonds with our children; it's the minor details that build profound relationships.

2. UNLOCKING OUR CHILD'S POTENTIAL

This chapter explores the intellectual needs of children aged eighteen months to three years, emphasizing the importance of nurturing their innate qualities. We'll discuss adopting both a proactive and creative stance in our daily interactions, ensuring a balance of lightness and engagement. Reflecting on my time as a teacher, I remember the profound connections formed between children and adults through the sharing of knowledge. This has led me to prioritize learning opportunities in my educational approach.

Understanding intelligence

The topic of enhancing children's intelligence often doesn't receive the attention it deserves. While we're inundated with advice on managing behavioral issues or engaging in play, the conversation rarely extends to fostering children's actual capabilities. This oversight might stem from many adults not fully recognizing what children are capable of achieving from a young age. Our children have vast, often under-stimulated, cerebral capacities that go unnoticed in daily life. Whether at home or in daycare, the activities offered to children frequently don't align with their true abilities. This misalignment can lead to astonishment when a young child performs a simple act, such as cleaning up a spill at two years old—a task that becomes straightforward when they've learned the principle of "*if you spill, you wipe.*"

We often underestimate our children's capabilities, either because we think we can do tasks better ourselves or because we believe the tasks are beyond them. This underestimation prevents us from recognizing their true potential.

My philosophy is in line with Maria Montessori, who advocated for providing children with learning materials suited to their age and actual abilities, proving that children are far more capable than we often give them credit for.

The Montessori method

Montessori classrooms are known for their higher achievement levels compared to traditional settings. It's not uncommon for a five-year-old Montessori student to read as fluently as a six-year-old in a conventional first-grade class. This success is attributed to Montessori educators who encourage the development of reading skills early and naturally, without dampening a child's enthusiasm for learning, even at four years old. The mixed-age classroom environment, accommodating children from three to six years old, allows each child to progress at their own pace, fostering an atmosphere of mutual assistance and individualized learning.

This child-centric approach is also beneficial for children who are homeschooled or whose parents emphasize informal, flexible learning opportunities. Traditional educational systems seldom encourage young children's curiosity about reading or subjects deemed suitable for older students. This reluctance often arises from the challenge of addressing diverse knowledge levels within large groups, leaving many educators uncomfortable with and unprepared to manage these disparities.

The right approach to learning

The notion that children should "just be children" and not be pushed to develop cognitively is a belief held by some adults, including professionals. However, my experience has taught me that leaving the transmission of knowledge solely to schools is far from ideal. With a functioning brain eager to explore, why not facilitate our child's venture into the realm of knowledge as their interest dictates?

This was a lesson I learned early on with my daughter, around six months old, when I began introducing her to simple problem-solving activities and impromptu learning sessions. I quickly discovered she was fully capable of understanding and responding to these challenges without the need for specialized materials. My aim was to cultivate a playful yet thoughtful intelligence, evident in our everyday interactions.

By consistently reviewing and adapting our interactions, I introduced more opportunities for her to engage in playful yet thought-provoking activities. For example, demonstrating object permanence by hiding an item and encouraging her to find it not only taught her that objects continue to exist even when out of sight but also fostered physical movement and a deeper connection between us. Although I share this story from when my daughter was still an infant, this method can be tailored to suit all developmental stages of a child.

For our Wonderful Twos, their brains are buzzing with activity, brimming with untapped potential despite their tender age. Our role is to gently guide and optimize these abilities, focusing on the process rather than the outcome. This approach ensures that learning complements, rather than competes with, the essential aspects of family life, offering suggestions that the child can freely explore.

Ideas to stimulate your child

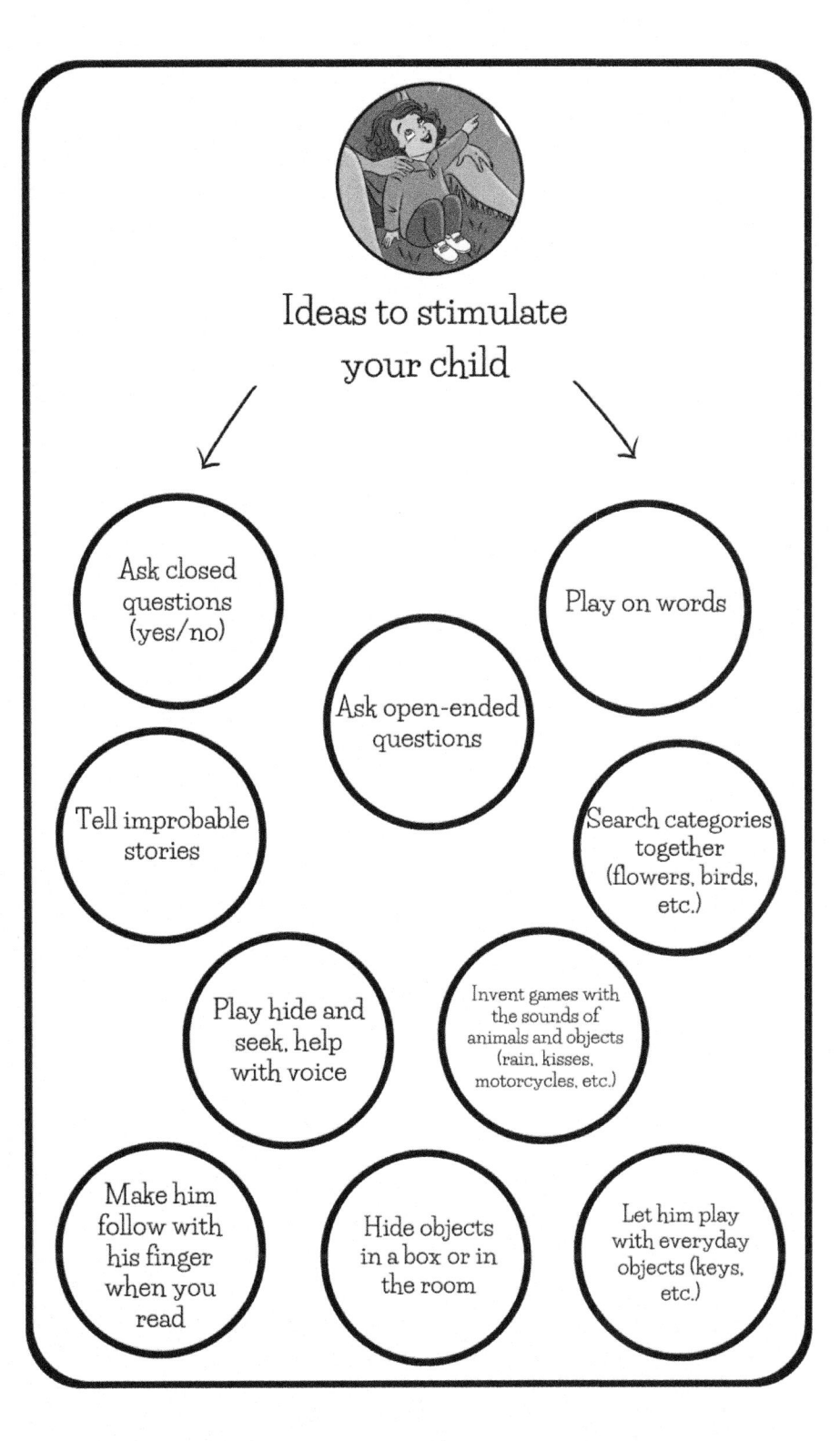

- Ask closed questions (yes/no)
- Play on words
- Ask open-ended questions
- Tell improbable stories
- Search categories together (flowers, birds, etc.)
- Play hide and seek, help with voice
- Invent games with the sounds of animals and objects (rain, kisses, motorcycles, etc.)
- Make him follow with his finger when you read
- Hide objects in a box or in the room
- Let him play with everyday objects (keys, etc.)

Language development

Between the ages of two and three, children become highly receptive to humor, nursery rhymes, wordplay, language, and interactions with adults around them. Words are a new and intriguing source of interest for them, not only because of their sounds but also as a means to soon express themselves more clearly. Typically, a young child understands everything, even if they can't yet articulate their thoughts. It's crucial to speak to them correctly, avoiding baby talk, to preserve a sound foundation they can mimic later when ready. For instance, when encountering a kitten, instead of saying, "*Look, a baby cat,*" we might say, "*Look, that's a baby cat, called a kitten. Do you want to pet the kitten?*" This approach greatly increases their chances of expanding their vocabulary when the time comes.

Giving them time to respond

We often rush to act or answer for our children when they're not quick enough. However, for their language and cognitive skills to flourish, children need time to think, to process situations, and the words used. This is how they'll find their own way to respond, be it through a gesture, babble, or word. Occasionally, ask your child a question and then pause. This necessary break allows them child to find the words or a way to respond. Regularly posing questions significantly aids in developing their linguistic abilities.

"Would you like milk in a glass or a cup? Are you still hungry?"

Then, let them respond (if they can verbalize) or show their choice by reaching for the item they want to use. You can then ask more open-ended questions:

"Did you play with Naomi or Liam today?"

Encourage them to respond, stimulate conversation, have them repeat phrases, and rephrase correctly if needed.

Enriching vocabulary

Day-to-day, it's beneficial to draw your child's attention to the objects around them, naming them as you point: "*a tree, a falling leaf, the office chair...*" These language moments also provide shared joy. Picture books are a valuable resource. These books primarily contain images with the word written beneath, sometimes accompanied by a few sentences describing the image. I prefer photos or illustrations that closely resemble reality, as many modern materials feature crude, computer-generated drawings that don't reflect the actual appearance (characters with oversized eyes or in fantastical settings, unrealistic colors...). Too playful drawings might distract from their initial learning objective: to know, recognize, and name new objects. When looking through a picture book with your child, point out familiar objects and introduce them to new ones. It's fascinating to later see their excitement when they recognize an object from the book in real life.

"Look at that insect, we saw it in the book last time, remember? It's a grasshopper! Can you say 'grasshopper'?"

Children speak when ready

Children may start speaking early, but there's no set rule. Each child is unique, and that's perfectly fine. There's no need to worry if your child isn't speaking by two or two and a half years old. They'll speak when ready; don't rush to consult a specialist. Trust them. My children began to speak quite well around twelve months and were forming complete sentences by two years old, although they started walking later than average. Some believe that when a child starts speaking, their focus shifts to this new skill, possibly delaying others, such as walking. If your child understands most of what you say, it's likely just a matter of time and confidence. Speech will come naturally. It's rare for children to have language disorders, so don't worry. Continue to engage in normal conversation, stimulating their language and vocabulary. Eventually, you might even wish for a mute button!

Using humor

Even very young children grasp humor well, which aids in developing their cognitive skills. Create humorous situations: hide something behind your back obviously, ensuring your child sees, then pretend you've lost it, exaggerating if needed.

"Oh no! My pen's gone again! Did you see someone take it?"

Your child will immediately look behind you, and you'll share a laugh at the situation. Next time, search frantically for your glasses, which are on your head, for guaranteed laughter. These seemingly simple scenarios engage various cognitive processes in a child's mind. Humor can also defuse many situations. If your child spills something and it's not a big deal, use a light tone:

"Oh my, there are corn flakes everywhere! What if I step on them and make it worse? Oh dear, what should we do?"

Hearing this, your child will naturally fetch a dustpan or their small broom, happy to help clean up.

"Phew, thanks for the great idea!"

Instead of creating a tense situation, you've used humor to encourage your child to correct their mistake. Another trick, especially during lengthy meals, is to place food in front of them and say:

"Whatever you do, don't eat this, okay?"

Then pretend to look away. Naturally, your child will take the "forbidden" food and eat it. Pretend to be upset or unaware of where the item went. Young children love feeling in control of our reactions, a rarity in their daily lives. The "Peekaboo" game, where we cover our eyes, is beloved because they can elicit specific emotions from us, a power they rarely have.

Find daily opportunities to infuse humor and camaraderie with your child, beyond just linguistic stimulation. Family time often leans towards the "serious" side. We're tired from our days and expect our children to eat quickly and behave until bedtime. While understandable, incorporating a bit of whimsy into our routine keeps the emotional connection within the family strong. These extra minutes can create joy in our families!

Invented stories

To add creativity to our days while stimulating our children, we can invent short stories featuring the child, a friend, or family members as protagonists. Whether set at the market, the beach, or atop the Eiffel Tower, the aim is for the child to dive into a semi-familiar world through the known character while immersing in fantasy. This nurtures their imagination and vocabulary, enhancing quality time with a parent.

I've done this with my three children as soon as they grasped word meanings. Sometimes, I'd ask them to suggest a character, place, or action for me to expand upon, letting my ideas flow freely. What joy! Later, as they grow into language, they can start inventing their own stories, further developing their vocabulary, language skills, sentence structure, and imagination. This enriching exercise can sometimes replace bedtime stories. Offer your child a choice:

"Tonight, would you like a story from a book or an invented one?"

Reading books to your child strengthens their language skills, comprehension, and vocabulary. It's beneficial to set up a reading nook early on, with a small box of books and some cushions on the floor. When your child shows signs of boredom or excessive energy, suggest they visit their reading nook. Once they start using words, show them the difference between text and illustrations. Use an adult book, like a novel, and challenge them to find the pictures, helping them realize adult books often lack illustrations.

Introduce the concept of authors and illustrators by reading a book's title and adding:

"Look, this book was written by So-and-So. This person wrote the book, and another person did the drawings, named Someone Else."

There's no need to elaborate; the goal is to plant seeds in your child's mind that will sprout over time and with future opportunities.

Introduction to letters: my approach with my daughter

Without aiming for specific outcomes, but through play and my approach as a mom (and teacher!), I taught my daughter the entire alphabet by age two. This exploration, guided by my pedagogical intuition rather than a formal method, isn't the only or recommended way to introduce reading, but it was a fascinating experience. By age four, she began combining letters. The goal isn't to push the child or race towards efficiency but to allow them to partake in the wonderful adventure of words and engage with their surroundings. We're surrounded by letters, and the objective is to show our children what they represent at the right moment.

Around eighteen months, I started with foam letters in the bath, one at a time, ensuring they matched the shape of our block capital letters. Alongside the foam letters, I pointed out letters in her reality, like on book covers. To her, a letter was just another object. Like a boat in her bath, there was an A, nothing more complicated.

Add variety to the child's daily activities

Incorporating exercises into daily life, I'd spontaneously draw animals or objects for her to recognize, sprinkling in letters. She quickly understood they belonged to the "letter family," as a zebra belongs to the animal family. I introduced new letters in her bath as she mastered the previous ones, eventually moving beyond the alphabetical order to isolated letters in our daily life.

By two, I wrote her name on frequently used items. At two and a half, I taught her to spell her name like a nursery rhyme, continuing with improvised letter games. Gradually, I explained that letters make sounds, finding objects that started with those sounds.

Though I was once a first-grade teacher, I wasn't familiar with Montessori's approach of teaching letter sounds before names. While logical, explaining the difference between a letter's name and sound suffices. The key is to introduce letters playfully, ideally before kindergarten, to avoid the pre-first-grade stress that often overlooks fun.

Follow your desire

As these examples show, there are endless ways to stimulate our children's lives. While there's no obligation to introduce them to letters or numbers, if you're inclined, follow your instincts. Even though my approach is influenced by my teaching background, I believe any parent eager to share knowledge with their child will find their own authentic method.

Ultimately, stimulating our children from a young age not only fosters their curiosity but also encourages them to find their own answers. My children are older now, but I still respond to their questions with, *"Can you figure out the answer yourself?"* They often do.

Developing children's intelligence is more about teaching them to think and find solutions internally than about knowing how to count to a hundred or recite the alphabet at two. If children easily retain information, it may benefit them later, but rote learning doesn't develop the same skills as constructing a thought process, something they'll seldom learn at school.

It's so good Mommy! Did Grandma cook it?
Well, I'll take that as a compliment...

Fostering independence

Children need to feel useful and find meaning in their actions, starting from a very young age. A child can become independent by the age of two if guided appropriately. This approach serves multiple purposes: teaching motor skills early on, instilling a sense of utility, and enabling them to manage everyday tasks. The key is to trust them, accepting that they may take more time, create a bit of a mess, or cause some initial chaos. Gradually, as you assist them in refining their movements, you'll find it saves time in the long run. Like anyone, children need to experiment to improve their control over movements, making experimentation a crucial phase. Though this phase might be uncomfortable for us as parents, it's essential. Walk through your home and consider what tasks or activities your child could perform in each room if you showed them the steps. This sensory connection with objects and daily actions truly brings meaning to their efforts, helping them feel more in place and somewhat in control.

Kitchen activities

The kitchen is an excellent playground and experimentation field for children, provided you've explained the tasks to them beforehand. Compile a list of kitchen tasks your child could perform:

- Peeling bananas,
- Cutting them with a child-safe knife,
- Peeling an egg, washing lettuce,
- Putting away groceries (like pasta packages or canned goods in the appropriate cabinet).

There's a wide range of tasks suitable for a Wonderful Two! These tasks will also develop their fine motor skills, crucial for precise hand and finger movements, which will be beneficial when they start to write. Initially, introduce activities under adult supervision. Show the child how to perform the task, not just by explaining, but by demonstrating the actions slowly. Conclude by asking if they've understood and if they'd like to try.

Gradual progression

Patience and kindness towards your experimenting child are vital. There's no need for complicated activities. Folding napkins and wiping down the table are excellent tasks for children, without needing anything more elaborate. The process of making our children independent also frees up our time. Gradually, we can trust our child with assigned tasks, feeling secure in their safety. This allows our child to stay busy while we engage in our activities. Of course, we won't stray too far and will check in occasionally to ensure everything's going smoothly. Autonomy activities can become shared experiences with our child or opportunities for them to grow, understand, and take pride in their accomplishments alone.

In the following page, you'll find ideas for everyday activities you can propose to your child. Feel free to add your suggestions based on what your living environment offers. Remember, an activity can vary in complexity, so tailor them to your child's abilities first and foremost.

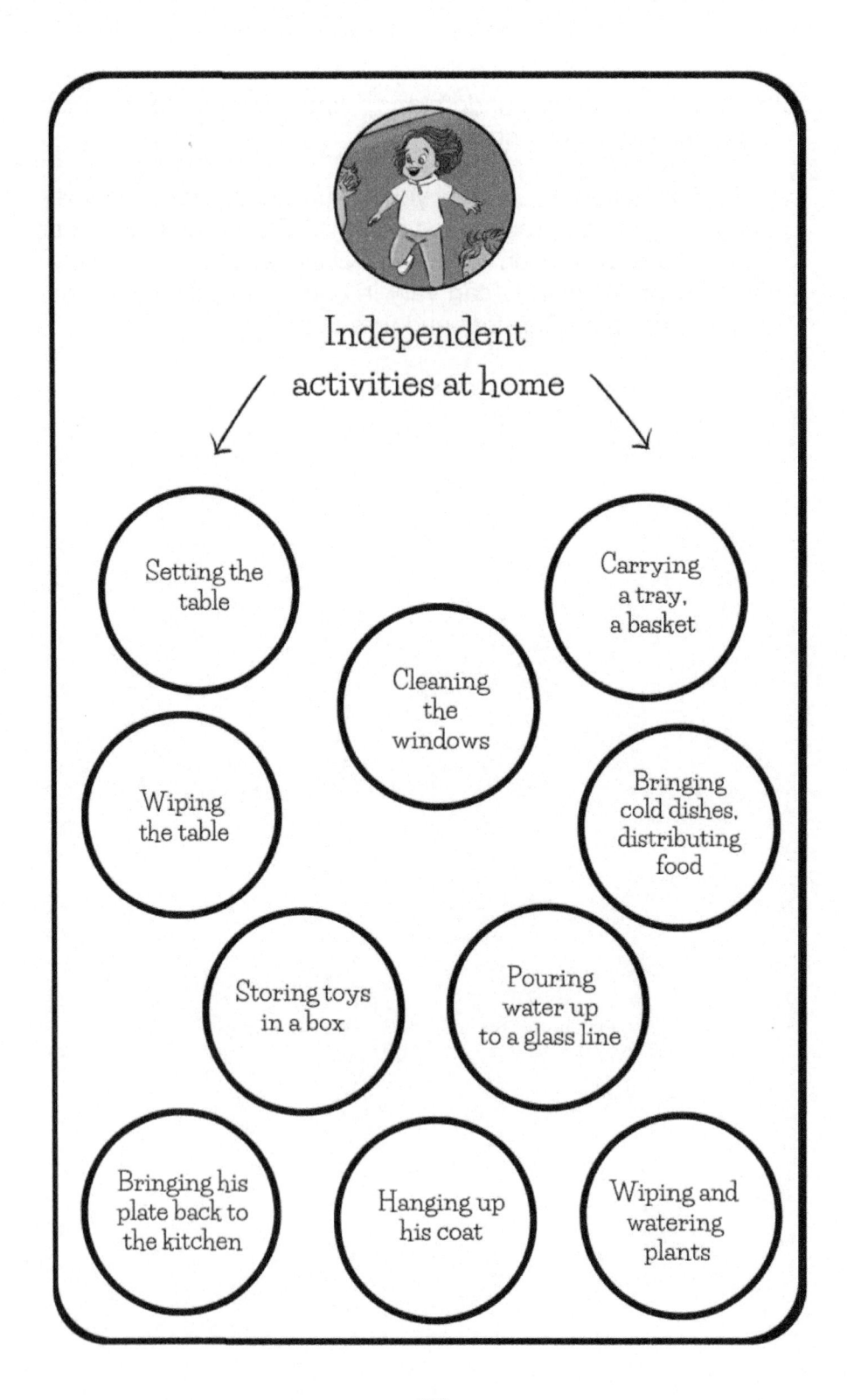

Independent activities at home

- Setting the table
- Carrying a tray, a basket
- Cleaning the windows
- Wiping the table
- Bringing cold dishes, distributing food
- Storing toys in a box
- Pouring water up to a glass line
- Bringing his plate back to the kitchen
- Hanging up his coat
- Wiping and watering plants

Sure, but what about the mess?

When your child spills water while attempting to serve themselves or drinks messily, guide them on how to clean up. In general, every slip-up should lead to an opportunity to "fix" the situation, with adult support when necessary. Adopting this mindset early, staying calm, and viewing these incidents as learning opportunities rather than annoyances allow our child to develop in a positive environment. The cause-and-effect principle of "I spill = I clean up" might seem straightforward to us as adults, but often, parents end up tidying up after their children. By encouraging our child to take responsibility for their actions and learn from small mistakes, we empower them. I use the term "mistake" lightly here, as it's a term adults often use to describe children's actions, though I personally avoid calling any child's action "silly."

Setting up accessible tools

Around the home, such as near the kitchen, consider setting up a child-friendly area like a low cart or the bottom shelf of a cabinet with utensils for eating, drinking, and cleaning independently.

Consider including:
- 2 plates,
- 2 glasses,
- 2 sets of cutlery,
- 2 fabric napkins,
- 1 placemat marked with spots for each utensil, if you're teaching table setting,
- 1 dishcloth for doubling as a bib or wiping spills,
- 1 sponge,
- 1 water pitcher for self-service...

I advocate for sustainable materials such as:

- Metal for cutlery, suitable for children or adults, with a slightly serrated knife that actually cuts, unlike typical blunt children's knives. A 350 ml metal pitcher can serve as a child-friendly pitcher. Metal glasses also prevent breakage.
- Fabric for dishcloths and napkins.
- Glass for glasses, chosen with care. Teaching your child to handle glass items gently can mitigate accidents. Glasses with a heavy base are ideal to reduce tipping. Importantly, avoid showing anxiety about potential breaks or scolding for accidents. If concerns persist, explore other options.
- Porcelain for plates, conveying that it's breakable. Where possible, choose durable, shock-resistant varieties.
- Melamine (sturdy plastic) is widely used for its affordability and durability, though personal preference varies.

The rationale behind these choices is that children don't necessarily need separate utensils from adults. By explaining the fragility of glass and porcelain, children learn to handle them with care. However, if you sense your child isn't yet ready for this lesson, it can wait. While plastic doesn't offer an optimal solution compared to natural materials, it's all about finding the right balance! At our home, we prioritize sustainable materials but have a few plastic items, and that's okay! The key is feeling confident in your choices.

Lastly, exploring the variety of materials used in kitchen utensils can become an engaging activity with your child:

- What's this material?

- Can it break?

- Do we have other items made of this material at home? (like a glass vase or metal bowl)

You might not delve deep into this until they're older, but it's a great way to start.

Develop fine motor skills

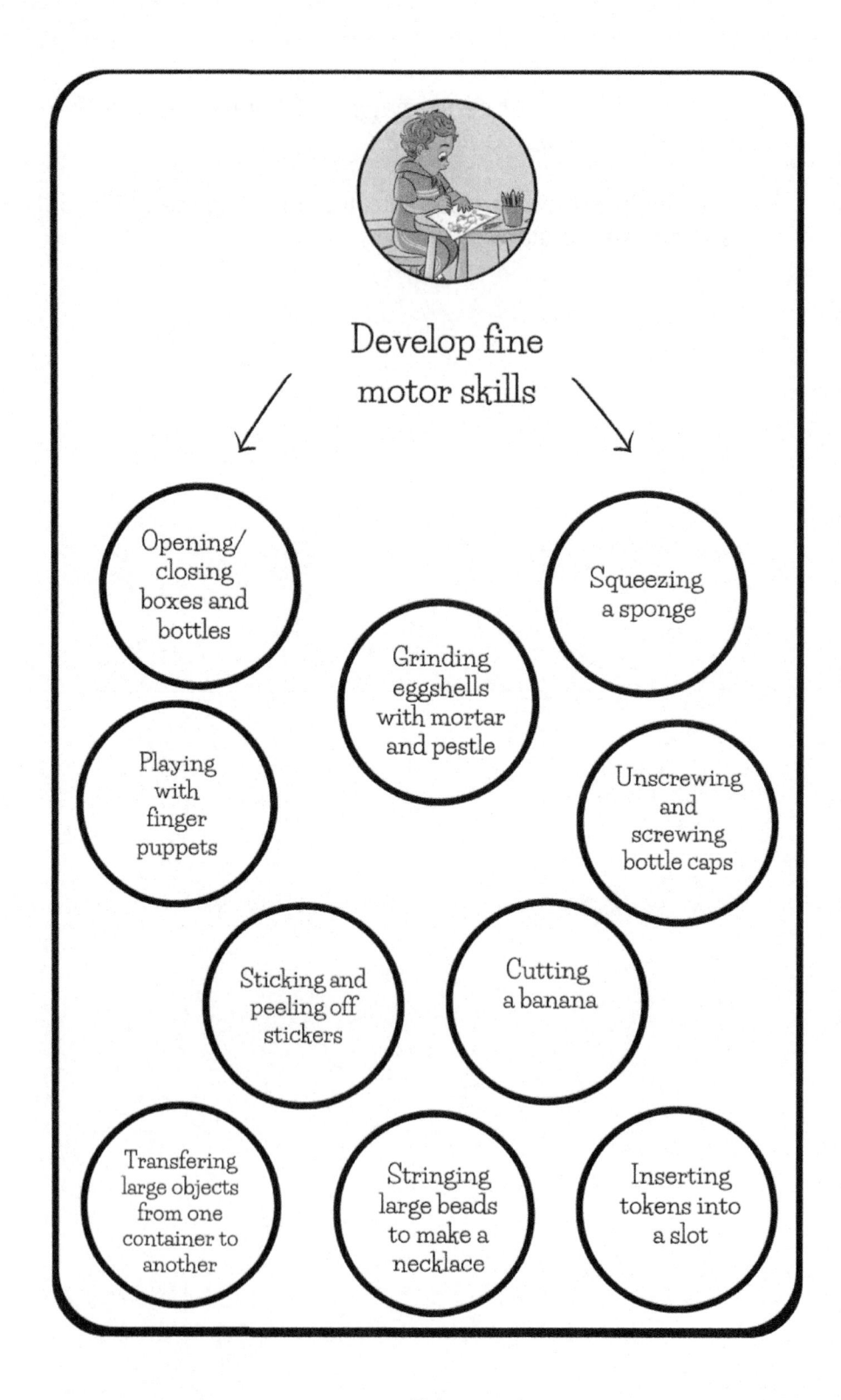

- Opening/closing boxes and bottles
- Playing with finger puppets
- Grinding eggshells with mortar and pestle
- Squeezing a sponge
- Unscrewing and screwing bottle caps
- Sticking and peeling off stickers
- Cutting a banana
- Transfering large objects from one container to another
- Stringing large beads to make a necklace
- Inserting tokens into a slot

Sensory exploration

As parents, we often hesitate to let our children touch things or put them in their mouths, worried about messes or potential dangers. Yet, this instinct to touch and taste stems from a fundamental need for sensory experiences. Maria Montessori recognized this, incorporating a comprehensive sensory learning section into her educational approach. Montessori education involves activities that engage all five senses, as she observed that children absorb knowledge more deeply when learning through sensory experiences. This concept is quite intuitive. Consider participating in a cooking workshop; replicating the dish becomes more intuitive and confident than merely reading a recipe. You connect with previously experienced sensations, enabling you to replicate techniques more accurately. Experiencing with our senses allows us to feel and deeply understand the situation, object, or context, fostering a more profound comprehension. Similarly, children can more easily grasp cause-and-effect relationships because they've physically experienced them.

Learning through sensations

The classic example of a baby's reaction to tasting a lemon for the first time speaks volumes. Without prior knowledge of its sour taste, a child will eagerly bite into it, quickly learning from the experience that lemon tastes unpleasant, likely deterring future bites. Had we cautioned, "*Don't bite into the lemon; it's sour,*" beforehand, the lesson wouldn't have been as impactful.

Touch plays a vital role in the development of toddlers. We should encourage them to explore as much as possible, allowing them to experience different textures, and distinguish between sensations like cold and warm, or smooth and rough. This exploration not only broadens their knowledge and vocabulary but also enriches their sensory memory, helping them differentiate between various textures and sensations. Creating sensory learning opportunities is simple. For instance, let them immerse their hands in flour while baking, or pour oil into their hands to mix — such interactions with different textures can be delightful. Kneading dough is another activity that offers immense satisfaction, allowing children the joy of getting their hands messy without fear of reprimand. Experiencing the transformation of ingredients into a tangible product firsthand is truly magical. Your child will beam with pride when sharing their hands-on achievements with family members.

Expanding sensory experiences

Introduce your toddler to a wide range of smells around him, from the fragrant to the foul. This approach can significantly sharpen their olfactory senses, a development I've witnessed in my own children. Encourage them to use their senses more actively by having them close their eyes and guess what you're placing in their hands, turning sensory exploration into a playful game. Isolating senses in this way can enhance their understanding of their environment. Simple, everyday activities like feeling the chill of ice cubes or the texture of tree bark offer rich, accessible sensory experiences.

It's crucial to remember that firsthand experiences, felt and processed through our senses, aid in memory retention, replication, and comprehension much more effectively than mere verbal instruction. That's why enriching your child's school learning with hands-on, experiential activities at any age is beneficial. When it comes to subjects like math, for instance, physical manipulation of objects can cement concepts more solidly than abstract paper exercises.

Sensory activities

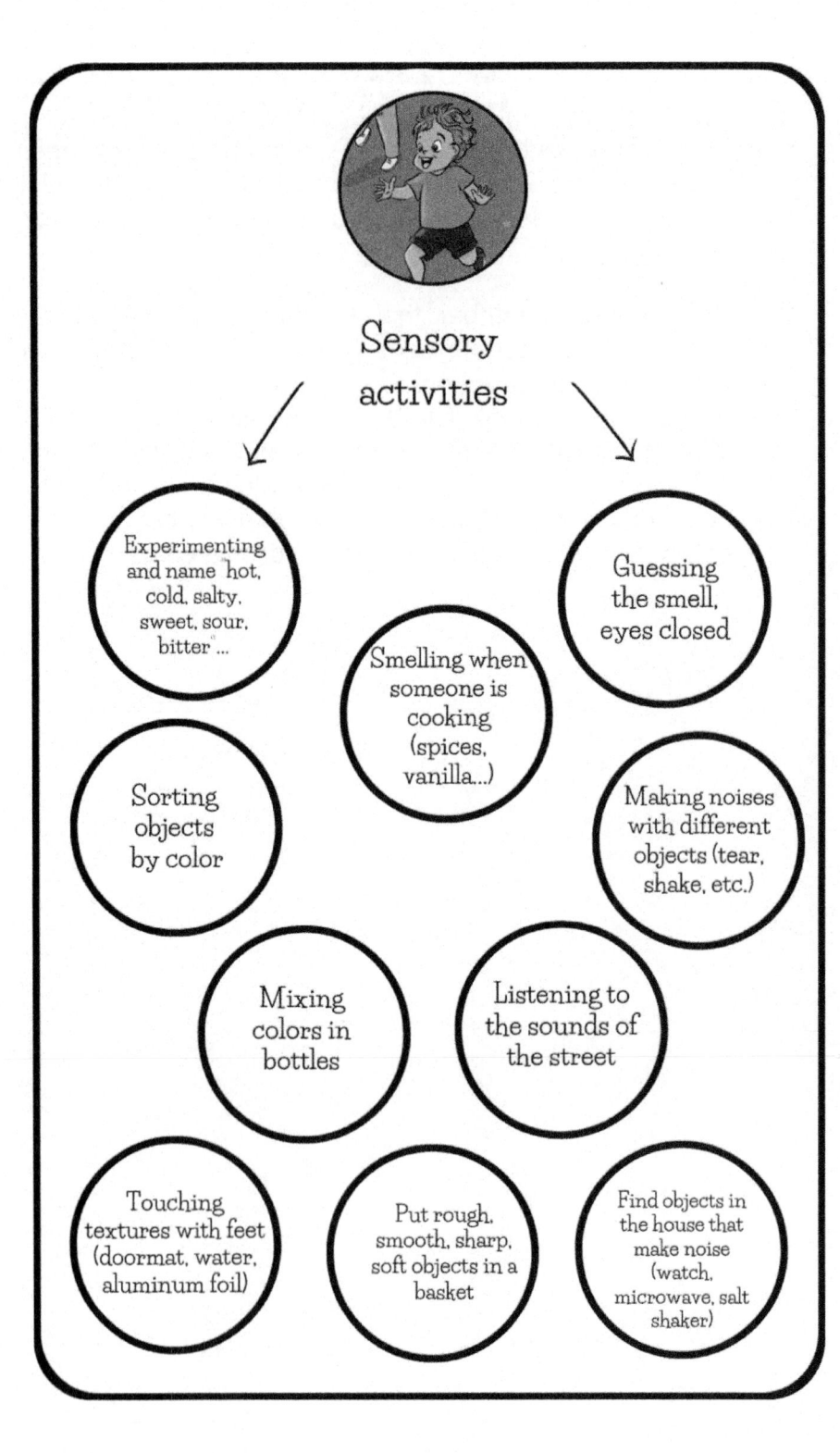

- Experimenting and name "hot, cold, salty, sweet, sour, bitter"...
- Smelling when someone is cooking (spices, vanilla...)
- Guessing the smell, eyes closed
- Sorting objects by color
- Making noises with different objects (tear, shake, etc.)
- Mixing colors in bottles
- Listening to the sounds of the street
- Touching textures with feet (doormat, water, aluminum foil)
- Put rough, smooth, sharp, soft objects in a basket
- Find objects in the house that make noise (watch, microwave, salt shaker)

Teaching self-management

Alongside sensory exploration, we can guide our little ones towards managing themselves in certain scenarios. This means showing them how to operate independently without our intervention when possible. The more a child understands the world and the objects around them, the better equipped they are to navigate it alone. Our goal as parents isn't to oversee every action our child takes—safety considerations aside. As Maria Montessori put it, our role is to aid the child in learning. Part of our mission as educators is to foster independence in our child, building their confidence and mastery over their actions. Here are a few scenarios where I've encouraged my children to manage on their own, despite their young age.

Distinguishing hot from cold

With my babies, I introduced the concept of hot and cold, always with a focus on safety. I found they could gauge the proximity to danger, like scalding water, through their senses. Here's how you might introduce your child to this concept:

In the shower, run cold water. Place your child's hand under it and say, "*Oh, that's cold!*" Your facial expression should emphasize the coldness. Switch to warm water, ensuring it's just above lukewarm.

Place their hand under the warm water and say, "*This is warm, even a bit hot, but it feels nice!*" Smile to convey the pleasantness. Then, slightly increase the water temperature—always within a safe range—and quickly remove their hand if it gets too warm, explaining, "*That's too hot! We need to be careful not to burn ourselves.*"

Switch back to cold water, reassuring, "*Phew! Now it's safe to touch; it's cold water.*" Repeat this exercise on another day, reinforcing the lesson with questions like, "*Should we touch very hot water? No, it's dangerous, we have to be careful!*"

This way, your child learns not to touch hot water to avoid burns. When preparing a bath, it's best to run the water when your child is nearby rather than in advance. Explain, "*We won't use water that's too cold or too hot to avoid burns. Let's find a nice, warm temperature.*" This helps your child grasp the concepts of hot, cold, scalding, and warm, making them more cautious when encountering similar situations alone.

Exploring temperature contrasts

This temperature exploration can extend to objects, like a metal spoon. I recall letting my coffee spoon cool to just above warm before placing it on my child's hand or cheek, a sensitive area.

I'd say, "*Feel how warm that is?*" Sometimes, I'd repeat with a room-temperature spoon, asking, "*Is this warm?*" to which my child would respond, "*no.*" This contrast helps children understand nuances in sensations, offering a deeper level of comprehension accessible through experimentation and explanation. When children feel discomfort from excessive heat, they naturally want to avoid it, understanding the risk involved. In the kitchen, explain that ovens, stovetops, and kettles are hot and off-limits to prevent injury.

Calm explanations based on temperature nuances make it easier for children to adhere to safety rules than simply shouting a warning without context. However, it's crucial to remember that children under three require constant supervision, even at home. The goal of this approach is to involve the child in their safety actively, but it doesn't replace the need for adult vigilance.

"Each year in the United States, 2,300 children younger than 15 years die from unintentional injuries in the home. More than 3.4 million children experience an unintentional home-related injury each year." (*Home Safety Program - Nationwide Children's Hospital*)

Exploring object textures

An interesting approach involves letting a child encounter potentially sharp or pointed objects rather than immediately reacting with alarm or envisioning danger. Similar to the hot water experiment, the goal is never to cause pain. The principle here is that preparedness to touch or feel something specific almost eliminates pain because we anticipate it.

For instance, you could introduce a toothpick or a sharpened pencil to your child by saying, "*Do you know what this is? It's a pencil. It's sharp at the end.*" You can lightly press the tip on your finger and say, "*Ouch, that's sharp! But it's okay, I didn't press hard, so it doesn't hurt!*" Then, you might suggest to your child, "*Do you want to try, very gently? Give me your finger.*" Lightly prick their finger to let them feel a slight sharp sensation and explain, "*See, it's sharp, isn't it? But if we press too hard, it can really hurt, and it could even poke our eyes if we're not careful. Do you know what else can hurt? Knives! Knives are sharp and can cut because they have a blade. They hurt our fingers. They're very dangerous for children, which is why we must not touch knives. Do you understand?*"

Next time you use a sharp knife, remind them, "*Remember how I told you that knives, like pencils, are sharp and can cut deeply? We won't try it because it can hurt and it's dangerous. Should children touch sharp knives? No, it's dangerous. Little children shouldn't touch knives, scissors, sharp pencils, anything that can cut or poke our eyes.*"

Explaining and allowing children to experience things firsthand helps them truly understand the danger because they've felt it. In daily life, seize opportunities to reinforce what they've learned by asking questions like, "*Can we touch water when it's very hot? No, because it can burn us, and it hurts. Can we touch a knife as a child? No, it can cause a lot of harm!*"

Exploring what goes in the mouth

Particularly before the age of three, it's understandable to worry about children swallowing small objects. It's natural to be concerned when they handle such items in unfamiliar spaces or without close adult supervision. However, there's also a way to teach them what not to put in their mouths without getting upset. This involves everyday learning, similar to previous examples. Constantly reacting with anger, fear, or impulsiveness won't help your child assess the seriousness of a situation through your tone.

Staying calm and only raising your voice in genuine danger alerts your child immediately, helping them steer clear of harm. I encourage visiting websites focused on choking prevention, which can advise on particularly dangerous foods and objects, how to minimize risks, and how to respond in emergencies. Additionally, knowing first aid seems essential for parents of children under six.

How to proceed?

Firstly, minimize the chances for your child to come into contact with small objects. This precaution can save a lot of worry. However, there might be times when we're less vigilant, visiting friends, or have older children who've left small toys around. If your child uses a pacifier, consider giving it to them during play to prevent them from experimenting with their mouth. Before they begin playing, explain, "*See this? It's a tiny object and dangerous because we could choke on it. We mustn't put it in our mouth. No, no, no! Do you understand?*" If they can respond, they'll nod or say "*Yes.*"

Stay calm and close without being overly anxious. If you're visiting friends, for example, it's better to stay near your child rather than joining adults on the couch. This prevents the need to constantly yell, "*Careful! Don't put that in your mouth! It's dangerous!*" or to snatch objects away abruptly. This method doesn't help children grasp danger as they receive too much unexplained information.

Instead, stay close, and if you think they might put something in their mouth, gently grab their wrist (without hurting them) and say firmly, "*No, no, no! We can't eat this; it's not food. It's not for eating. It's dangerous because we could choke!*" Use facial expressions or gestures to reinforce your words. Continue this throughout playtime, consistently using the same words and expressions to say, "*No, no, no!*" You might also use a finger wag or a cautionary look. This approach worked well with my children. Keep such interactions brief to avoid overwhelming them, despite its importance for safety. If possible, divert their attention to another toy.

Creating a catchphrase

Later, reinforce understanding by asking, "*Can we eat small toys? No, no, no! Can we eat bread? Yes, bread is for eating. Well done!*" This consistent approach helps children recognize the difference. They may even look to us for approval before putting something in their mouth. Initially, you might test them by presenting a small bead and a piece of apple, asking, "*Can we eat the apple? Yes!*" Exaggerate your approval to aid their understanding.

"*Can we eat this bead? No, no, no! It's not for eating; it's dangerous!*" Encourage your child to mimic you, saying "no" with a gesture indicating danger. These repeated words and gestures become a refrain for your child in potentially dangerous situations. Remember, a child's brain is developing, and repetitive situations become reflexive, turning repeated phrases into mantras.

Teaching the concept of time

It's well known that our children, especially the very young ones, lack patience. They live in the moment, desiring immediate gratification. The concept of time is abstract to them. Telling our Wonderful Two to "*Wait five minutes!*" or asking, "*Can't you wait just two seconds?*" is beyond their comprehension. When we say, "*We'll buy a croissant tomorrow,*" or "*We're visiting grandma in two sleeps,*" it seems straightforward to us but often isn't for them. They grasp that it won't happen now but lack an understanding of the precise reason or the duration of the wait.

For a child desiring something, waiting five minutes or two days feels almost the same: too long. The concept of time is seldom addressed with young children, yet understanding it can significantly improve our interactions with them. Rarely do we take the time to explain this concept, yet a child who grasps it can better manage their frustration.

Providing concrete examples

From the age of two, we can help our child start to navigate the concept of time, to gauge durations, and to understand what constitutes a long or short wait. This enables them to anticipate events and manage their daily lives better. As mentioned, at this age, children struggle with self-control, leading to frustration, tantrums, and anger. The idea is to anticipate and provide tangible tools for better understanding their world, offering experiences and nuances. Like in many scenarios, dramatization, miming, expressive gestures, and facial expressions can greatly aid in illustrating differences between moments.

For instance, to convey "*now*," we might point downwards, emphasizing, "*We're playing with this game right now. This instant!*" To explain "*tomorrow*" or "*later*," we could gesture forward with our hand, saying, "*This is tomorrow, this comes later*," or emphasize the first syllable: "*This is tomooorrow, this is laaater*," pairing gestures with vocal emphasis.

Two minutes vs. ten minutes

Demonstrating the difference between two and ten minutes can be enlightening. Two minutes is relatively short, while ten minutes can feel lengthy to a child, especially depending on the context. Try this: sit with your child, start an activity, and after a moment, look into their eyes and say, "*I'll be back in one minute, I need to...*" Choose something simple, like, "check if I put my keys in my bag."

Indicate one minute with your index finger, telling your child, "*I'll return in a minute, wait for me here*," and then leave the room. Ensure your child stays put or stops to wait for you. During this time, narrate your actions aloud, "*I'm reaching the kitchen. Ah, found my bag! Just checking for my keys. Ah, there they are, coming back!*" Upon returning, affirm, "*See? I was gone for a minute. Great waiting!*"

Starting with one minute is crucial, but we often tell our children, "*Wait two minutes!*" It's less common to say, "*Wait one minute!*" So, later, experiment with two minutes, explaining this will take a bit longer. "*I'll be back in two minutes, can you wait?*" Don't view these exercises as trivial or time-wasting, as they save time and energy by helping your child understand time durations. I've tested these methods on my three differently-tempered children, and each time, they've quickly grasped the difference between two, ten, and even five minutes.

Making it a habit

This is all about consistency, habituation, and repetition. Systematize the process using gestures, dramatization, or repetitive phrases to embed a routine. Just as saying "*Goodnight, my love, see you tomorrow,*" signals bedtime to your child, we're creating similar mental "routines."

When you leave for two minutes, initially comment to reassure your child, making the wait seem shorter. For example, halfway through, you could say, "*I haven't found what I was looking for in my bag yet. Hang on a bit more. You can keep playing; I'll be right back.*"

Regularly practicing the two-minute exercise ensures your child understands the concept. Gradually, they'll learn what "waiting two minutes" means because you've also used it in various daily situations. "*Two minutes, just need to speak with dad,*" "*Let's draw for two minutes!*" Soon, you'll find yourself moving away from saying "Wait two seconds!" as it becomes meaningless and potentially confusing for your child since we never truly wait just two seconds.

The five-minute test

Using a song can make the five-minute test easier. Find a song about five minutes long and tell your child, "*I need five *minutes to prepare your bag for tomorrow. While I'm gone, you can listen to this song. It'll make waiting easier. The song lasts five minutes, so I'll return when it ends."*

This exercise is more effective if they can start the music themselves. *"As soon as I leave the room, press play, and when it stops, I'll be back. Ready?"*

Ensure you return precisely as the song ends. After practicing the two-minute and five-minute exercises, your child will understand the difference. *"Remember, two minutes isn't very long. It's like when I was finding my keys. Five minutes is a bit longer, like when we listened to the song last time."* Soon, you'll only need to reference these terms without needing examples

Varying durations

As your child grows, introduce them to longer time periods, such as ten minutes, by engaging in an activity with two consecutive five-minute songs playing in the background. During daily routines, specify the duration when asking your child to wait. For instance, *"Our turn at the doctor's will be in ten minutes."* As they mature, their understanding of time will become more nuanced. You can then introduce even longer durations, like thirty minutes, explaining, *"Thirty minutes is a long time. It's like how long we stay at the park after school."*

Always relate the duration to a specific activity or moment to help your child grasp the concept of time. Thirty minutes at the park may fly by, while the same amount of time spent in line at an amusement park or ice cream stand may feel endless. Time, however, is not subjective but a precise unit of measurement. This is a conversation worth having with your child.

"Have you noticed how sometimes five minutes can feel very quick when we're doing something we love, but really long when we're not enjoying ourselves? Yet, five minutes is always five minutes. It feels too short or too long, but the same amount of time has passed."

Morning and evening

By around three years old, once you feel your child has a good grasp of time, you can extend to longer periods, like morning and evening. "*In the morning, we do this and this,*" and "*In the evening, we do this and this,*" using examples from their daily routine. You might also introduce the days of the week, even if they don't fully understand yet. My approach, regardless of the goal, introduces a subtly increased level of difficulty, allowing the child to engage with new information when ready.

If you decide to display the days of the week, take an A4 sheet placed horizontally and draw a simple chart with seven columns for the days and split the rest into morning and evening. Write the days in capital letters from Monday to Sunday. Use tokens of two different colors to represent home and school, affixing them with adhesive putty. Place the chart at the child's eye level in the living room or their bedroom, and regularly point to the chart, saying, "*Look, tomorrow is Wednesday. Will you go to school tomorrow? No, see, it's not blue, meaning no school and you'll stay home with me.*"

Of course, adapt this to fit your child's life and activities. By gradually and repetitively introducing these concepts over several months, you'll significantly aid your child in understanding various durations, shedding further light on the world around them.

What equipment to buy for our child?

Becoming a parent often comes with the temptation to purchase a plethora of baby gear: the latest, most convenient stroller, the chic yet expensive changing table... With the arrival of our child, we naturally want to create a comfortable environment and might think acquiring a full set of parenting paraphernalia will make our lives easier. However, I've found the opposite to be true: the less we buy, the simpler daily life becomes. This applies not only when the baby arrives but also as they grow. In many families, we observe that an abundance of furniture and objects often complicates maintaining order at home. Anticipating these issues by thoughtfully considering what is truly worth purchasing is wise, especially since children grow quickly and there are alternative ways to acquire items, such as borrowing from relatives, buying second-hand, etc.

Some considerations

Firstly, transitional objects like sippy cups for transitioning from bottles to regular glasses, or training toilets before using the actual toilet, are best avoided. After bottle-feeding, offering a child a glass with a slightly heavy base will help them adjust. If the goal is for them to drink from a regular glass, bypassing an intermediary step is preferable. Similarly, special plastic cutlery for children isn't particularly useful. It's better to opt for small metal utensils that children can learn to handle. There will always be an array of unnecessary gadgets tempting us, like suction-cup plates to prevent spills. Often, these items end up forgotten in a cupboard; it's easier just to skip them altogether. Teaching children to use everyday objects can lead to mastery within weeks.

Choosing a bed

For young children's beds, several options are viable, and here are my thoughts on some. Cribs can be controversial, as some believe they make children feel "caged." I used cribs for my three children, removing one side when they began to climb out, without feeling they were "imprisoned," but rather secure. However, I understand this may not suit everyone. A mattress on the floor allows the child to go to bed and get up as they wish, promoting freedom of movement. This is often recommended in Montessori education for fostering independent mobility.

However, this setup, while natural and simple, might not fit seamlessly into every family's lifestyle. For example, it could lead to a child who constantly joins their parents in bed or doesn't feel tired at bedtime, disrupting morning routines. Finding a balance between providing a safe environment and ensuring adequate sleep for the family can be challenging with almost unrestricted freedom of movement. If this option interests you, I suggest trying it for a week or two, keeping an open mind about whether it suits your family. You're not obligated to anyone.

As you can see, I'm not dogmatic in my choices, relying more on intuition and the realities of modern life. While I'm drawn to a wholly natural approach and home education, I can't ignore the logistical, emotional, and financial implications of these choices. Hence, I encourage making educational decisions free from the pressure of any particular educational philosophy or societal expectations. Don't feel compelled to adopt every aspect of Montessori education if it interests you, nor should you feel trapped into a consumerist approach to toys and equipment if you're curious about exploring other methods.

Listen to your intuition. There's merit and demerit in everything. This mindset allows me to balance nuances and values that resonate with me and my family without fear of making mistakes. This reflection extends beyond educational materials to screen time management, dietary habits, and more. Everything is about balance and consistency. Some may advocate for a "pure" approach, believing a method only works if fully embraced. While I respect this viewpoint, it might be too rigid for some parents and children.

Returning to bed choices, an interesting alternative is a toddler or travel bed with a standard child's mattress, manually removing one side of the fabric. This allows safe entry and exit while still offering the structure's coziness. Another long-term solution is a "big kid" bed with a rail to prevent falls. Ultimately, don't overcomplicate things. The priority is for your child to feel safe, comfortable, and for the arrangement to work for the whole family.

Other equipment ideas

- For meals, consider a booster seat that fits over an adult chair instead of a bulky high chair, allowing the child to join family meals at the table. Replace the booster with a cushion as they grow.
- A "learning tower" or a sturdy two-step stool, preferably wooden, with protective sides can safely

elevate your child to participate in kitchen activities or other household tasks at counter height.
- In the child's bedroom, try to avoid an overload of toys (more on this in the next chapter) that can overwhelm rather than aid in play choice.

If you want to create a play area in the living room, clearly define it and use a box for easy cleanup post-activity.

Useful material

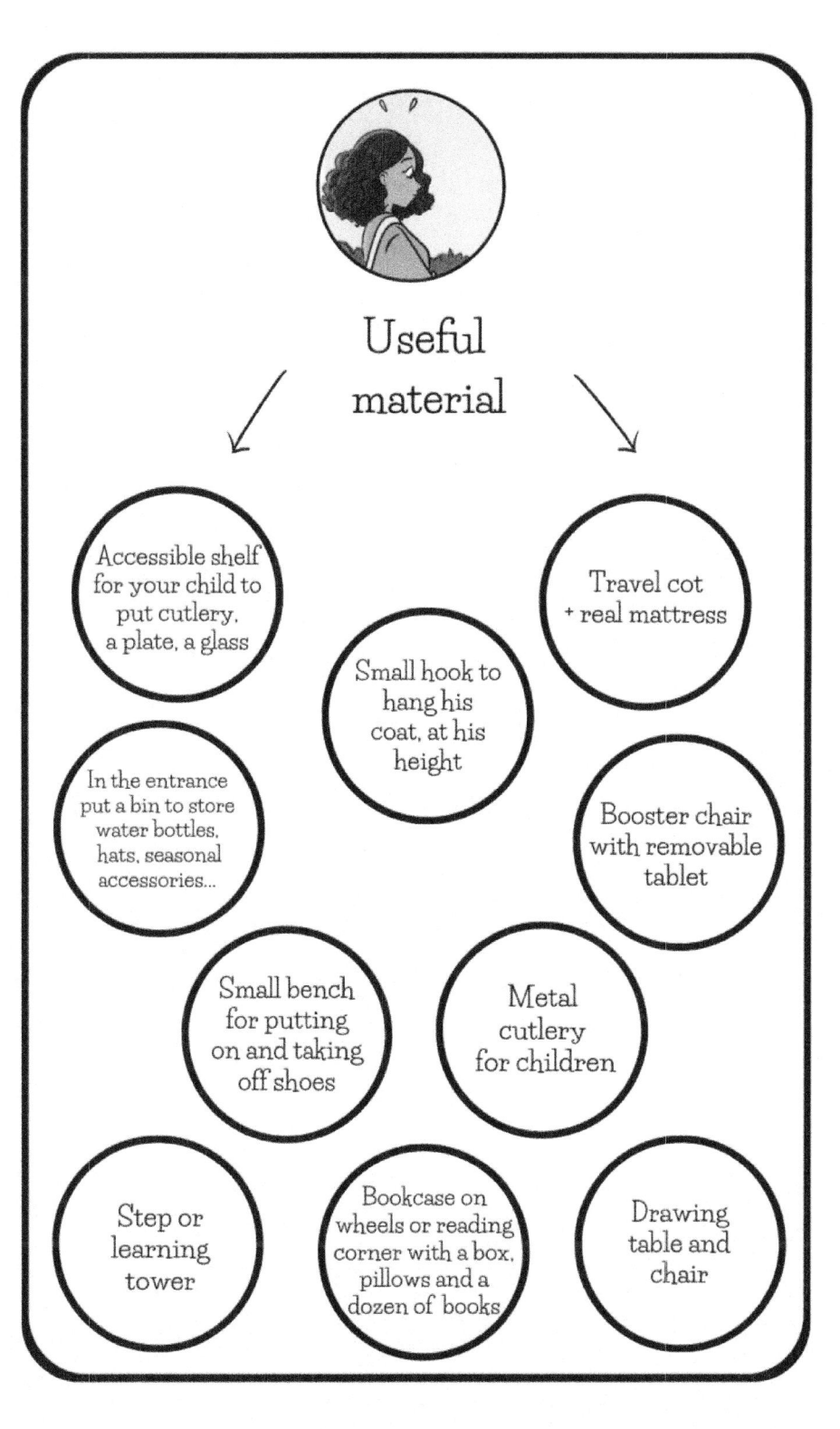

- Accessible shelf for your child to put cutlery, a plate, a glass
- In the entrance put a bin to store water bottles, hats, seasonal accessories...
- Small hook to hang his coat, at his height
- Travel cot + real mattress
- Booster chair with removable tablet
- Small bench for putting on and taking off shoes
- Metal cutlery for children
- Step or learning tower
- Bookcase on wheels or reading corner with a box, pillows and a dozen of books
- Drawing table and chair

Preferred toys

From eighteen months to three years, children enter a new phase of exploration and interaction with toys. This period is ripe for experimentation, as they are undergoing significant cognitive and physical developments:

- Language development,
- Vocabulary acquisition,
- Improved gross motor skills,
- Refined finger dexterity...

Here are some tips on which materials or approaches to prioritize:

- As recommended by the Montessori approach, opt for noble and durable materials like fabric, wood, and metal in the child's environment. Choose toys made from these materials over plastic, which is increasingly common today. Natural materials not only connect the child more closely to their environment but also tend to last longer.

- Everyday objects can serve as fascinating playthings: a colander with spaghetti to thread through its holes, a slot in a formula box for inserting coins, an old wallet for inserting and removing cards, magazines for tearing up or making collages…

- Regarding commercially available games, the ages indicated by manufacturers are merely suggestions. The same toy can engage both a baby and a three-year-old if adapted to their abilities. Likewise, games intended for children over six can be offered to your Wonderful Two with altered instructions.

Here are two examples of how to adapt the same toy to fit a child's capabilities, sometimes repurposing them entirely:

- A Memory game can be used as intended for older children. For younger ones, it can serve as a portable image gallery to enhance vocabulary. Another idea is to hide the cards in a toy with flaps and ask the child to find specific ones.

- With three baby toys, you can take turns hiding them around the room and guide your child with hints like "*no, that's too far!*" and "*yes, you're getting closer!*"

Always tailor play situations to your child's abilities, not their age. It's normal and okay for children not to be able to do the same things at the same age. The most important thing is to be attentive to the skills they're developing at their own pace, rather than comparing them to a presumed age standard or to other children.

Everyday objects

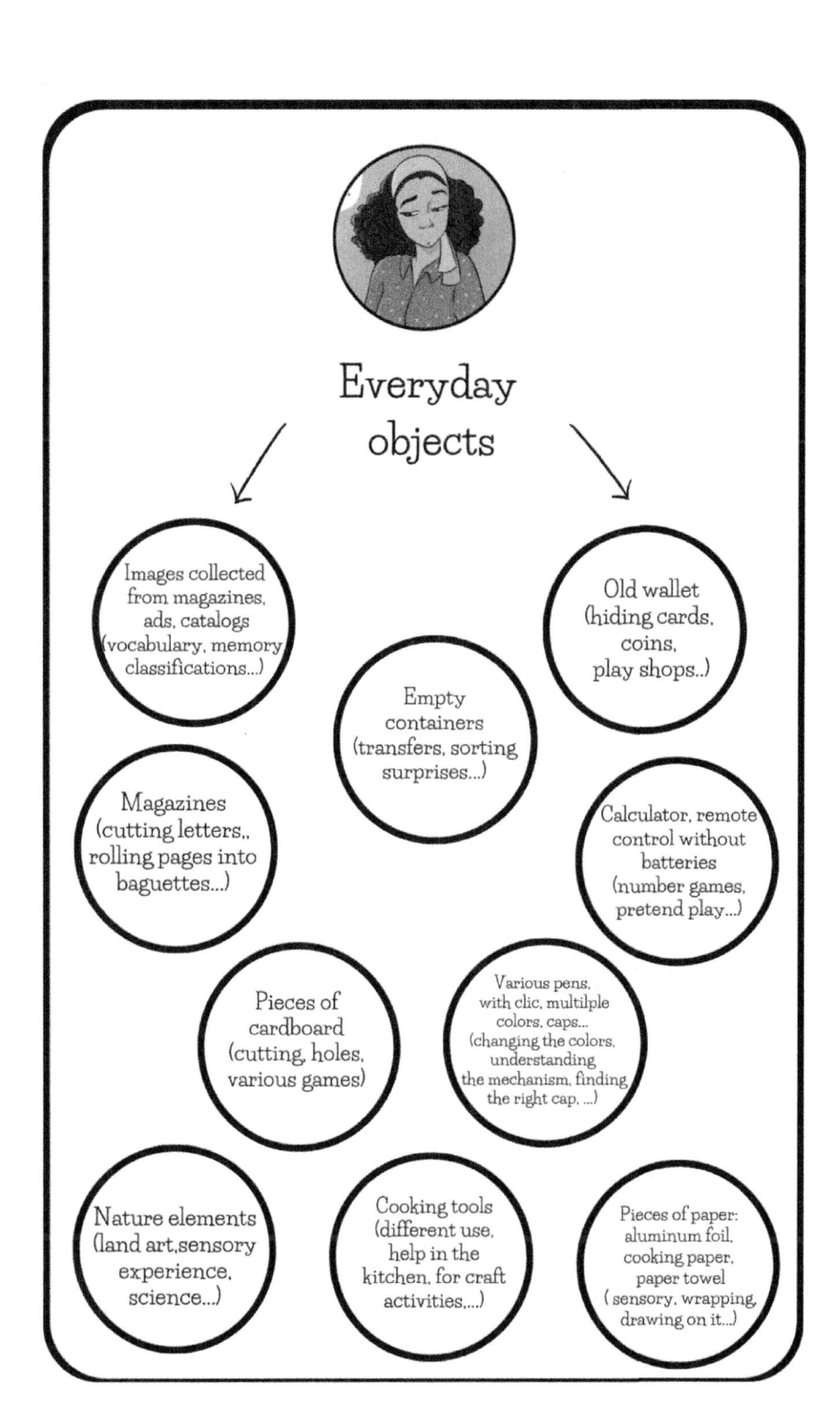

- **Images collected from magazines, ads, catalogs** (vocabulary, memory, classifications...)

- **Old wallet** (hiding cards, coins, play shops..)

- **Empty containers** (transfers, sorting surprises...)

- **Magazines** (cutting letters,, rolling pages into baguettes...)

- **Calculator, remote control without batteries** (number games, pretend play...)

- **Pieces of cardboard** (cutting, holes, various games)

- **Various pens, with clic, multilple colors, caps...** (changing the colors, understanding the mechanism, finding the right cap, ...)

- **Nature elements** (land art, sensory experience, science...)

- **Cooking tools** (different use, help in the kitchen, for craft activities,...)

- **Pieces of paper: aluminum foil, cooking paper, paper towel** (sensory, wrapping, drawing on it...)

It's essential to pay close attention to your child's unique behaviors. If you notice anything amiss or have a gut feeling that something is off, it's crucial to investigate further, even if it means seeking external advice. However, in most cases, children simply require more time to adapt, and it's important not to overreact. Just as walking is a milestone every child will eventually reach, they will similarly develop and refine various other skills over time.

- In your child's room, aim for a minimalist environment, avoiding the clutter of too many toys. A tranquil setting with muted colors helps prevent the child from feeling overwhelmed.

- Young children don't need an abundance of playthings at once. Implementing a "toy rotation" strategy can keep their environment fresh: showcase a selection of toys while storing others away. Rotate these toys monthly, based on your observations of their preferences, to keep their interest without overwhelming them with choices. This prevents confusion and indecision, common in children bombarded with too many options. This strategy is effective for children at all developmental stages.

Choosing effective educational tools

- According to the Montessori method, select tools designed for a single learning goal. A tool for learning letters, for instance, should not be colorful to avoid confusing the child with multiple learning objectives.

-
- Avoid overly noisy toys, as they can create a subtle, continuous stress. Instead of toys that operate purely on button presses for action or sound, consider options like a set of wooden musical instruments. This encourages the child to be an active participant in their

learning and play. Alternatively, repurpose empty shoe boxes by filling them with household items or toys and seal them creatively for a unique play experience.

- While not toys per se, continuous background noise from music or television can overwhelm a child's cognitive processing. The inadvertent background noise might stem from a fear of not providing enough educational stimulation, yet it can lead to increased stress for both the child and adults.

- I discovered a range of toys perfectly suited to the development of toddlers up to 4 years old. These are the Play Kits from the American brand Lovevery available individually or as a subscription. The toys, classified by age group, are Montessori-inspired, made of wood with soft colors. They also include books about emotions and important moments in a child's life, counting toys, weather and season board, sensory activities, independent play... I had the opportunity to test them with my younger son and other little ones. As a teacher, I can only recommend them because of the numerous learning possibilities and the fact that they can be combined with each other. Each kit comes with a complete booklet for ideas to play with your child.

As a toddler expert, Lovevery asked me to represent the brand and to offer my readers an exclusive 40$ reduction with the code **LOVEDEBO40**. *(The currency adjusts depending the country but is equilvalent to 40 American dollars.)*

https://lovevery.com (USA and Canada)
https://lovevery.com.au (Australia)
https://lovevery.co.uk (United Kingdom)
https://lovevery.eu (Europe)

(Terms and conditions: Use the code LOVEDEBO40 to receive 20$ off a new Play Kis subscription (40$ off when you prepay for multiple game kits or 20$ off each of the first two game kits when you pay per kit). Valid for new subscribers only. Discount codes and coupons cannot be shared, are not transferable and cannot be exchanged for cash. See the FAQ page at https://lovevery.com/pages/help#faq for more details.)

This is the only partnership that I accepted among the many proposals I received because I really fell in love with these toys.

Designing for the child's perspective

Keep in mind that children experience their rooms from their own vantage point. Decorative elements placed beyond their direct line of sight might not enhance their environment meaningfully. However, decorating with family photos or art at the child's eye level can enrich their space personally and culturally. This also offers opportunities to discuss family memories or introduce basic art appreciation in a natural, engaging way. Always ensure that such decorations are placed where the child can easily see them, focusing on educational value rather than just aesthetics.

In essence, nearly anything can become a tool for play and learning. The key is to maintain a balanced approach without obsessing over constant efficiency. Each parent should find a balance that works best for them, embracing the flexibility that truly benefits daily family life.

Toy base

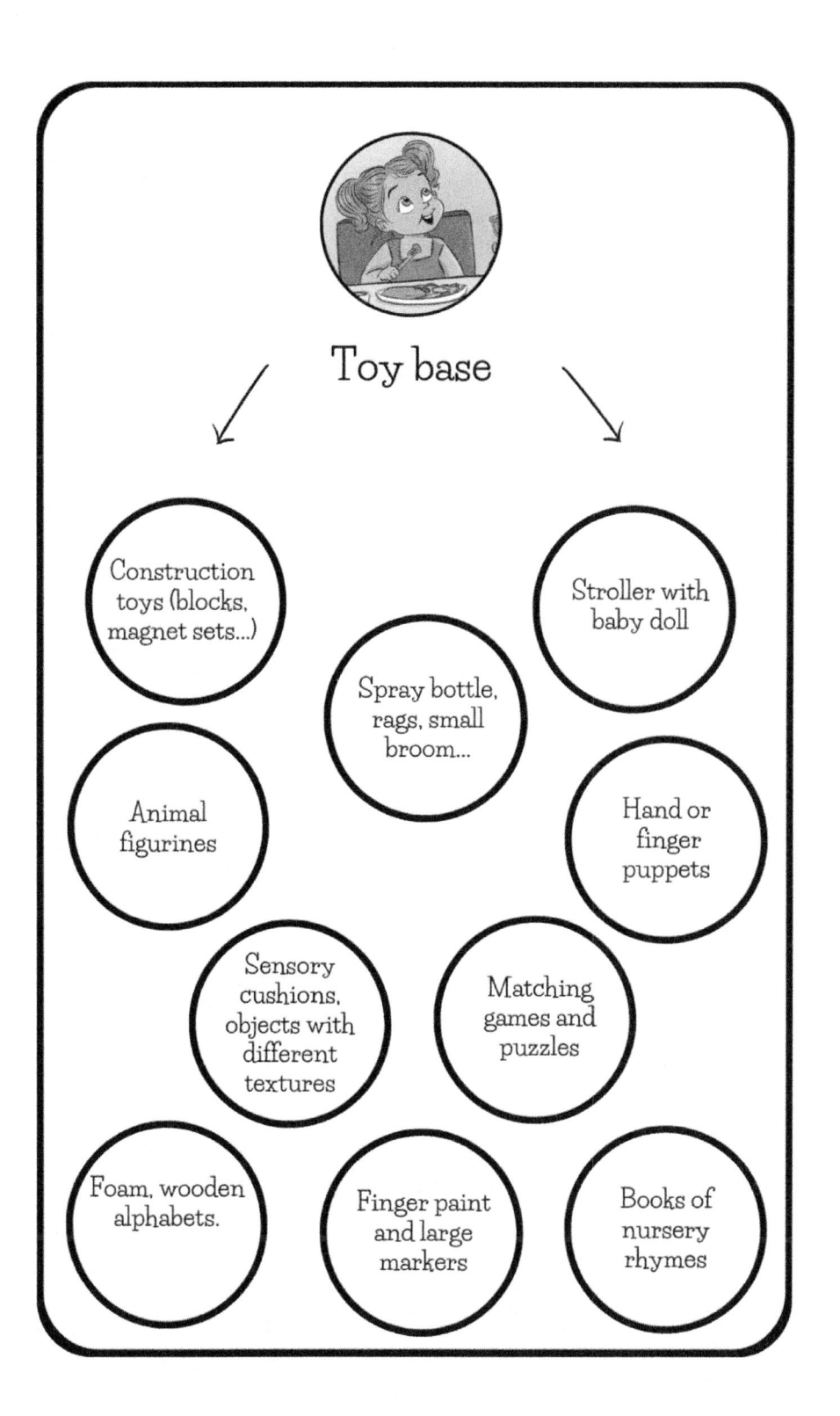

- Construction toys (blocks, magnet sets...)
- Stroller with baby doll
- Spray bottle, rags, small broom...
- Animal figurines
- Hand or finger puppets
- Sensory cushions, objects with different textures
- Matching games and puzzles
- Foam, wooden alphabets.
- Finger paint and large markers
- Books of nursery rhymes

3. MANAGING THE ENVIRONMENT, NOT THE CHILD

Let's delve into guiding our child's boundless energy and introducing them to societal norms. Although a two-year-old may not fully grasp social conventions such as manners, patience, or the concept of cleaning up after themselves, providing a clear and consistent framework is crucial for their sense of physical and emotional security.

Setting boundaries for reassurance

Many parents find it challenging to establish boundaries. Often, this hesitance stems from a misconception that a nurturing or "conscious" parenting approach means avoiding any confrontation with the child through limits or rules. On the flip side, some parents believe that strict boundaries are the key to maintaining control and asserting their authority.

However, a balance between these extremes is not only achievable but also vital for healthy development

Children inherently need boundaries to grow and feel secure. They rely on their parents to signal when they're pushing the limits too far, helping them understand the bounds of acceptable behavior. *"I'm exploring my world, and my parents guide me on what's too much. This helps me learn what's okay and what isn't."*

Yet, this doesn't imply a need for constant oversight or demonstrating power over our children by imposing arbitrary restrictions. From about eighteen months, children's exploration is essential to their development. Unnecessarily stringent barriers to this exploration can lead to frustration, either suppressing the child's personality or leading to more frequent outbursts. Thus, it's crucial to strike a balance that allows the child to freely express themselves while ensuring the well-being of everyone involved.

Boundaries must be clear

Creating boundaries within the home requires thoughtfulness and reflection because, while they may evolve, they form the educational foundation we pass on to our children. They delineate the space within which the child can grow, reflecting the values we hold dear. Yet, defining these boundaries concretely, to solidify the pillars of our family and provide a clear educational direction, is a step often overlooked. The limits we set need to be straightforward, equitable, and minimal. Children of this age don't grasp subtleties, exceptions, or contradictions.

Consider a traffic system with nuanced rules – it would be utterly unreliable:

"At a roundabout, give way to the right. Except when traffic is light, then just negotiate with the other driver."

The same principle applies at home: children need to rely on our words without any room for misunderstanding.

Therefore, we need to clearly articulate what is and isn't allowed.

General statements like "*We need to behave at home!*" are too ambiguous. Children can't decipher what "behaving" specifically entails. Instead, clearly defining an action leaves no doubt: "*Jumping with shoes on the bed is not allowed, got it?*" Confusion is virtually impossible with short, frequently repeated sentences. Generally, explaining or justifying a rule isn't necessary.

Boundaries must be fair

Fair boundaries mean they are universally respected and understood within the family. Discrepancies between parents' rules create confusion. It's imperative to reach consensus privately, not in front of the child. There's always room for compromise, and a flexible approach in parenting is often the most effective. Children inherently understand fairness and will accept communal rules when they see them as just and for the collective good.

Moreover, a fair rule remains consistent, not fluctuating with the adults' convenience. If eating on the couch is off-limits, adults should adhere to this rule, especially in front of the child. Otherwise, it's perceived as unfair and confusing. Young children struggle with nuances and exceptions, so we must model consistency in adhering to established rules.

Boundaries should be limited

Our Wonderful Two is in the throes of personality development and needs room to experiment. Constant scolding for minor misdemeanors like occasional couch-jumping, water spilling or finger-eating defeats the purpose. Choose your battles wisely and let minor issues slide to prevent unnecessary stress. This encourages us to rethink arbitrary limitations that seem to serve more as a control mechanism than genuine guidance. Often, such restrictions stem from our upbringing or a misunderstanding of children's needs. Refraining from imposing every possible prohibition isn't laxity but practicality. How often do we, however, hear parents setting needless restrictions?

Children are not mere extensions of ourselves but individual beings with age-appropriate curiosities. Our role as parents is to facilitate their growth, smoothing out their sometimes "wild" or abrupt behaviors, but we're not accountable for every action. If your child touches a vase at a friend's house, it doesn't reflect poorly on your parenting. You're the guardian of a curious being drawn to explore. Request your friend to secure the vase and redirect your child's attention. A handful of vital prohibitions are more than adequate for our children's development!

Setting clear guidelines

Let's get practical and define specific boundaries for your household by writing them down on paper or in a notebook. Remember, it's useful to revisit and adjust these boundaries as your child or family's needs evolve.

1. Start with physical boundaries. The physical safety of our little ones is our top priority, regardless of their cognitive development. You may feel a strong connection with your child and believe they understand everything, but this doesn't mean they can safely navigate potentially dangerous situations alone. Children do not fully comprehend danger until around three years old. Therefore, we must always be extra vigilant, both at home and outside. Begin by listing all potential hazards at home.
Examples:

- Cover sharp corners at the child's height.

- Keep sharp objects, medications, and cleaning products out of reach.
- Monitor access to stairs and elevators closely.

2. Identify external dangers. List potential dangers in places you frequently visit (parks, grandparents' homes, etc.). Anticipate these issues before each outing, like a faulty gate at the park or an unleashed dog at the grandparents' house. Remind your child of the rules regarding these potential dangers before heading out. Remember, physical safety rules are non-negotiable and must be enforced with kindness yet firmness if needed.

Examples:

- *Avoid sharp or pointed objects.*
- *Stay away from significant heat sources.*
- *Hold an adult's hand when crossing the street.*
- *Don't go beyond a certain tree at the park…*

3. Address easily resolvable concerns. Make a list of items with sentimental value or those too fragile. Also, note areas of the home where you prefer your child not to enter. Find permanent solutions for these issues.

Example: Place a cherished figurine out of reach, lock the home office.

4. Note common prohibitions. Write down instances where you typically forbid your child from doing something and actions that particularly bother you. For behaviors that are age-appropriate and will pass with time, consider whether they truly need to be prohibited or if they can be tolerated for now.

Example: If the child doesn't eat neatly, recognize it as age-related and avoid reprimanding.

Find practical solutions for other issues to reduce tension.

Example: Remove shoes upon entering the house to prevent couch stains.

5. Distract to avoid "don'ts". If, for instance, you prefer your child not to play with your smartphone, distraction with another object can be very effective at this age.

Don't ask for the impossible

The smartphone scenario is a compelling one because it might initially seem straightforward to restrict our "Wonderful Two" from using it. As adults, we understand the negative impact screens can have on young children, whose brains are still developing. We'll explore this in greater detail in the book's final chapter. Therefore, it feels natural to tell our child: "*No, no, no! You know you're not supposed to use mommy's or daddy's phone!*"

However, expecting a two or three-year-old to comply with this rule, while adults around them are almost constantly on their devices, doesn't make sense. Even as adults, who are fully aware of our actions, struggle to resist checking our phones at social events, we expect our toddlers to ignore an object that's a significant part of their surroundings?

How can a child, with their limited ability to discern nuances, distinguish between times when it's acceptable to watch a cartoon on the phone and times when the phone is off-limits, lying on the coffee table? How can they understand the difference between this "toy," which is sometimes allowed and sometimes forbidden, when all the toys in their room are always accessible? Do we ever consider things from our child's perspective to prevent unnecessary tantrums and frustration? Conclusion: if we don't want our child touching our smartphone, the simplest solution is to keep it out of their sight. This instantly solves the problem.

After considering this, there will be little left that we feel we need to forbid our child. Putting our thoughts on paper helps us gain perspective on daily irritations and understand that many are inconsequential. This process often liberates us from an authoritarian role that doesn't fit with such a young child. It also eases the pressure we feel around them, reminding us they're often incapable of controlling their impulses or being mindful of their actions. Ultimately, we provide our child with the physical and psychological space they need to grow more confidently.

Avoid saying "No!"

As observed, two-year-olds are naturally curious, drawn to follow their instincts. This innate curiosity is crucial and should be preserved. Our children aren't to blame for the size of our living space or our busy lifestyles. They need room to move freely and make decisions. Understanding our child's development makes it easier to avoid imposing unnecessary restrictions. While we must navigate the demands of our hectic schedules, it's important to ensure our child has ample freedom, as long as their physical safety is not at risk. The aim is for children to feel free within the home without being burdened by constant oversight. This approach was the foundation of the exercise I previously suggested.

Sacrificing (a little) adult comfort

Once established, we must remember our child is still learning: we should accept that our homes will often be disordered, requiring more cleaning and patience. All of this goes against our preference for an adult-organized environment! The "Wonderful Two" phase is temporary, and although our children may disrupt the cleanliness or tranquility of our homes until around age four, it's important to remember that this phase will pass.

Here are a few strategies to ease the process:

- Offering a drink can refine toddlers' fine motor skills, but to prevent spills, consider having them practice this in the bath.
- If our child tends to eat with their hands, placing a small tarp under their high chair or a placemat under their plate can be useful.
- A large bib or an adult-sized shirt can help minimize messes, and teaching our child how to use a napkin can be a valuable lesson.

There are always solutions to manage messes, but flexibility is key. I assure you, adopting this approach will make our child more adept in their movements and lead to a calmer phase around three to three and a half years old. Limiting restrictions in their early years has shown me that children develop sufficient freedom to practice, explore their environment, trust themselves, and refine their skills until three years old. By age two, they could eat cleanly, wash themselves, and manage simple tasks. By three, they were capable of pouring from a pitcher without spilling, cleaning up after themselves, and more.

This approach saved me significant time in the long run, proving that raising toddlers with constant commands and prohibitions, hoping they will respect their surroundings more, is misguided. Instead, allowing them maximum freedom, guiding them while ensuring their safety, helps them know themselves better from a young age and develop greater self-confidence.

Another method to "coexist" with our energetic little one is to involve them in our daily activities by assigning them a task or an object to "imitate us." Children love to mimic adults, so let's use this to our advantage! A memorable example for me involves my children watching me apply makeup in the morning. Their presence in the bathroom, their curiosity, and their occasional tugs for attention could make mornings challenging.

To manage this, I would give them a few harmless makeup accessories. Sitting on the floor beside me, they had access to blush and its brush, an eye pencil (with a broken tip), and a mirror that could be opened and closed... This way, they played at applying makeup like mommy (yes, with my boys too!), manipulating the mirror and pencil. I used these moments to teach them the names of different objects:

"This is mascara, but I won't give it to you because it's messy. It's used to make mommies' eyes pretty. Watch how I do it."

Adapt this strategy to other personal moments:

- Folding laundry = involve the child by having them match their socks or fold their small T-shirts.
- Assembling furniture = let them sort non-sharp accessories by category.
- Organizing cabinets = give them an empty box and some items to "organize" inside...

A child with engaged hands is far easier to manage.

They, too, love to say "No!"

As we try to limit the use of "No!" in our household, it's baffling to hear it frequently from our child! Indeed, our "Wonderful Two" often employs negation to express their desire for choice or to communicate disagreement. They're beginning to know what they want, setting mini-goals driven by their young minds, which naturally don't account for obstacles or potential consequences. These frequent "no's" are also messages the child sends to themselves as they begin to internalize the concept of boundaries.

Let's consider a specific example to better understand our little ones' refusals and how best to respond: Our three-year-old daughter is midway through her meal, sitting with us, when she spots a teaspoon on the table. It reminds her of the yogurt she recently enjoyed. Suddenly, she's overtaken by an irresistible urge for yogurt. She will express her desire with increasingly clear and emphatic requests. If possible, she'll head straight for the fridge, unconcerned about what's in her way, whether she's finished her main course or not. Thus, when we ask her to come back and deny her the yogurt immediately, she's likely to respond negatively.

« My darling, you haven't finished your meal; you can have yogurt afterwards! Come, sit back down!
— No!
— Yes! You need to finish your meal before having dessert, you know that!
— No, I don't want to! I want the yogurt!»

Typically, this is when tensions rise: we're irritated by the child's defiance, as it seems they're challenging our authority and doing as they please. We aim to model the correct behavior, with varying degrees of patience. For instance, we might pick up our little one as she struggles, shouting "No!" and place her back in her chair, whether she likes it or not. Another approach some parents might take is to send her to her room, telling her she needs to calm down and listen to her parents.

This scenario, while fictional, is designed for illustrative purposes, staying close to common situations while describing the reactions of a child in refusal and parents reacting in the moment. It could easily be adapted to any context where you've felt powerless or wished you had reacted differently. Let's try to approach things differently, aiming to reduce tension for the entire family, step by step. For clarity, I'll take on the role of the mother with my own daughter.

1. **Put yourself in their shoes**. My daughter is thinking about yogurt; she can't control her craving and isn't acting against me; she simply has no interest in the convention of "dessert after the main course." She's following her young impulse.

2. **Manage my emotion**. This essential perspective allows me to lower my guard, not to feel wounded in my authority or parental ego. Thus, I don't think, "She's testing me, I must not give in, she needs to know who's in charge!" These thoughts are actually meaningless, especially at this age. Being calm doesn't mean being permissive; on the contrary, it fully embodies our adult role and invites our child into a more peaceful interaction.

3. **Verbalize and offer a compromise**. With these considerations in mind, I would have let my daughter get the yogurt, helped her take it from the fridge, and said:

"Oh wow, that yogurt looks too tempting, doesn't it? You want some, right? But you know, you haven't finished your meal. Look. What should we do?... Ah! I know, let's taste a bit of the yogurt, but then we'll finish our meal, okay?"

This way, we find a compromise likely acceptable to the child while explaining our expectations.

4. **In case of refusal**. If she refuses, I'll need to find another approach based on the situation, such as distraction or a creative idea to move her onto something else.

Examples include:

- Suggesting she keep the yogurt next to her plate while finishing her main course and talking about something else,
- Setting a timer for five minutes to help her visualize the passing time while finishing her meal and focusing her attention on it,
- Asking her to close her eyes and guess what we're putting in her mouth, starting with the main course and moving to the yogurt as a reward.

5. **Anticipate next time**. Finally, in a calm moment later on, I would explain to my child that next time, it would be good to try and wait to have yogurt until after finishing her main course.

Some might think all these steps are time-consuming or impossible to implement in the heat of the moment. I completely understand. However, without recognizing that parenting is not a series of impulsive reactions from the parent to the child, the relationship becomes flat. Constantly lamenting a child's actions, focusing on every detail that seems to challenge our authority, leads to an "adult versus child" model, creating a perpetual power struggle.

Conversely, if we curb our initial impulses, take a moment before reacting, and realize that our child's "No's" are not personal attacks, we can foster a stronger relationship based on understanding. This is true at any age: we can step back and find strategies to avoid tension. Distraction, play, and humor are just a few options. With a proactive approach, we'll gradually become experts in managing "No's," effortlessly navigating these challenges.

How to speak to our Wonderful Two?

It's not always clear how to best communicate with our child, especially during challenging moments. Should we raise our voice, risking scaring them? Or remain neutral to preserve kindness, even in the face of their little "mishaps"? Often, our tone naturally aligns with our personality. Some parents adopt a firm approach when giving instructions, believing this will more likely lead to obedience. The issue with consistently using such a commanding communication style is a loss of credibility. This happens because our child, overwhelmed by constant directives, can't assess the seriousness of situations or prioritize information when their parents always use the same tone. A parent who frequently yells throughout the house to gain compliance will lack genuine communication with their child.

Conversely, some parents opt for a more relaxed, even monotone voice when communicating, even if the child's behavior is excessive or potentially dangerous. While this approach may seem to respect the child's autonomy, it has its downsides: it doesn't allow the child to understand that certain behaviors require immediate attention or are unacceptable. This could be problematic, for example, if a child hits a parent. In a passive/impulsive or permissive communication style, children may tend to disregard adult speech as insignificant, tuning it out over time. I believe there are pros and cons to every communication style. Thus, the goal isn't to completely abandon our natural inclinations but to find a balanced approach.

Using a firm tone

Firmness doesn't equate to yelling, anger, or authoritarianism. A firm tone is confident and deliberate, not about creating constant power struggles by raising our voice or shouting for every little thing. A firm tone can be akin to making eye contact. It conveys intention without instilling fear. However, an authoritarian tone might mean giving the child a stern look to evoke fear. We need to express nuances and firmness when necessary.

A firm tone is necessary when we believe our child is in danger or going too far in their actions, especially after we've already expressed our concerns and believe they're capable of understanding. In such situations, we must do more than give a defiant look or use a tone that frightens our child. A respectful day-to-day communication style, considering our Wonderful Two's desires, emotions, and needs, is preferable. A firmer tone can signal to the child that their behavior is inappropriate or dangerous. Establishing a balanced tone early in life helps them understand our expectations and limits. In reality, a firm tone is only necessary in immediate danger or when we sense the child has lost control over their behavior. The foundations we lay in early childhood will carry on, requiring less effort later as our child will understand us, sometimes with just a glance or a word, and quickly adjust their behavior. The toddler years are an ideal time to learn effective communication nuances.

Theatricalize when possible

When our child tries a new food, for example, we can nod to show approval and convey what liking something means. "You really like mango, don't you?" We might pat our stomach to show it's enjoyable. Theatricalization is an easy-to-use tool. When we don't want a child to perform a certain action, like putting an object in their mouth, we can simply say:

"*No, no, no!*" while waving our finger to emphasize the negation instead of yelling. This method is more impactful for the child as it includes a visual representation of our expectations. Initially, this might feel silly if we're not accustomed to communicating this way. Yet, incorporating theatricalization into daily interactions can enhance parent-child communication.

Exaggerating our message can minimize the words used, avoiding cognitive overload for our child, whose brain is constantly active. Some parents use baby sign language with pre-verbal toddlers, a method I find intriguing for fostering communication based on eye contact, gestures, body language, and non-verbal cues rather than bombarding our child with words they might struggle to process. Remember, the brain's numerous connections require time to integrate and utilize information.

Communicating without words

In Montessori pedagogy, conveying instructions in learning situations offers inspiration. Demonstrating to a child how to use materials can be done silently, except for specific terms related to the learning task. We show actions through slow gestures, speaking only when absolutely necessary for understanding. This preserves the child's thought process and minimizes confusion. This supports the idea that words are not always necessary for communication. In fact, the less we say, the more children can navigate their thoughts, use their brains, and reflect. As discussed regarding children's perception of time, they need time and silence to process information and respond, verbally or otherwise. Adopting the right tone with our children means finding a communication method that is respectful and effective for daily interaction while also able to convey necessary nuances when required.

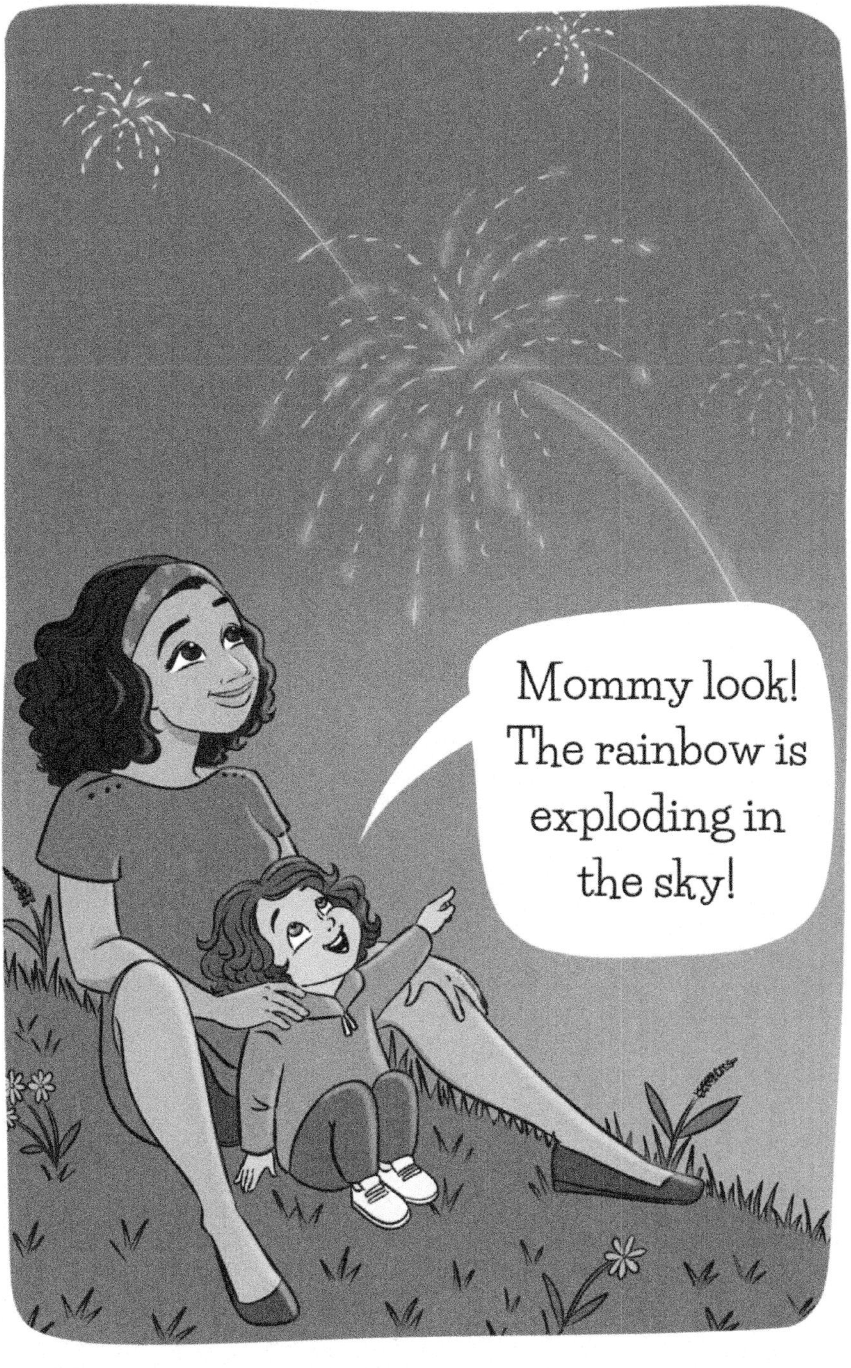
Mommy look! The rainbow is exploding in the sky!

Avoiding tantrums and managing emotions

If I haven't yet discussed children's tantrums even though we're past the midpoint of this book, there's a straightforward reason. My observation of this age group, through my experiences with my own children and in various childcare settings, is as follows: if we create an environment that fully addresses our child's needs in all their dimensions, tantrums will be exceedingly rare. However, according to proponents of the "Terrible Two" theory, tantrums seem to define this unique age. I hope to have shown you, through the various topics covered so far, that this portrayal of the small child as terrible doesn't align with reality.

I also hope you've realized that the term "Terrible Two" only considers a superficial aspect of a two-year-old's personality without offering any suggestions for improvement. This portrayal of the child as a wild creature who balls up at the slightest inconvenience overlooks the multitude of facets within them.

When we address all their needs—physiological, cerebral, psychological, emotional, etc.—they feel secure, and their behavior changes completely. Of course, like adults, a child at any age is influenced by different facets of their personality that emerge unexpectedly and must be addressed. Our child, like any human, constantly experiences emotions—highs and lows, euphoria, joy, excitement, as well as sadness, fear, confusion... Given their limited brain development, they simply can't control all these upheavals.

Tantrums are natural... for everyone!

While it's true that toddlers are more prone to express their emotional state through excesses or "tantrums," these are not inherently problematic. What matters is how we respond. It's normal for a child to cry, scream, flail about, or even roll on the ground occasionally. Our little ones struggle to control these outbursts; they lack the words to explain their feelings, the patience to wait, the strength to hold back, and the maturity to act reasonably. They experience constant frustrations that manifest as tantrums and screams, which often make us uncomfortable. Generally, we find it difficult to witness someone else's distress because we're unsure how to help or react. It's especially hard for a parent to see their child in such a state when all they want is their well-being. Yet, what the other person, adult or child, is experiencing is simply a temporary state. Our child is okay, but they need to express what they're feeling right now and without restraint.

The Wonderful Two isn't as mature as an adult.

In our adult lives, when we're hurt, for example, we don't burst into tears or scream. This is because we've experienced this before; we know how to put it into perspective, our brain is mature and signals that the pain will quickly fade. However, when our child experiences the same, their brain doesn't provide the same information. Rationality doesn't guide them, whereas the sensation and emotion associated with the potential pain, but especially the shock, are overpowering. They can't calm down on their own, but they know that we, the adults, and especially their parents, who are their closest emotional anchors, have the ability to soothe them.

This is evident when our child falls and isn't necessarily hurt but reacts based on our response. If we express concern, saying, "*Oh dear, that must have hurt!*" even if it didn't, they're likely to pretend to be hurt and cry for our attention. Conversely, if we simply help them up, saying, "*Oh, you must have been scared, but luckily it doesn't look like you're hurt!*" they'll carry on as if nothing happened. This shows that our reaction significantly impacts our children's tantrums or excessive behaviors.

Our role is to calm them during a meltdown.

Our little one needs to express their discomfort, essentially saying:

"*Calm me down as you know how. Help me manage what's happening in my head because it's too much for me!*"

That's what a tantrum signifies. A tantrum doesn't mean you're a bad parent, that your child is difficult, or that you're failing to meet their needs. It's merely information about a transient state they're experiencing. So, don't blame yourself when your child screams, is unhappy, cries, or when you don't understand them—it will pass. Don't think it's your fault. It's simply their brain trying to regulate itself amidst life's unpredictabilities. Of course, as we've discussed at length, there are ways to minimize our little ones' frustrations, but tantrums will persist, and the child must be able to express them without fear.

When a child has a tantrum his face usually turns red. We might consider this as a warning that we're going to be in charge of the emotional weight that our child cannot carry by himself. The red face is a signal that we have to take a breath and be ready to help our toddler.

Parents judge each other.

It's a fact; we parents often find ourselves observing other parents, passing judgment on their parenting styles. This usually serves to validate our own parenting approaches. It might seem trivial when written down, but it's the truth! Yet, we don't know what goes on in their homes. We witness a scene at the park where a mom scolds her child and deem her too harsh. We see a child joyfully rolling in the mud while their dad watches silently and label him as permissive. Do we know what these parents endure daily? What kind of upbringing they're providing for their child? Are we aware of their struggles, life choices, or the day's events? Just as we're clueless about their lives, other parents know nothing about ours when our child throws a tantrum. That's why we shouldn't feel ashamed when our child acts out in front of other adults who seem judgmental. And it's also why we shouldn't judge other parents! If uncomfortable, we can explain that our child is young and doesn't yet know how to handle their overwhelming emotions.

They're not having a tantrum to annoy us.

When in the midst of a tantrum, our child isn't trying to provoke us, test us, or push our boundaries. Yet, this is often what we're told:

"Ah, he's testing you! Don't give in! You have to show who's in charge!"

Our child is grappling with their emotions, feeling so uncomfortable in their own body, and we're supposed to assert our dominance to show we're "the boss"? No! They're simply experiencing life as a child with an immature brain that can't reason with itself! Their brain wants everything immediately and reacts impulsively—it's physiological! Therefore, we shouldn't be upset with our child for being in this state; it's not their fault either. We shouldn't react impulsively or arrogantly, trying to assert our authority through punishment, time-outs, louder yelling, or other power struggles.

Instead, as parents, our job, with children of any age, is to control our impulses to provide a reasoned and appropriate response they're incapable of finding on their own. If we try everything within our power to channel and temper the situation, with some practice, we'll manage to soothe most tantrums. Before offering specific examples on how to do this, I'll add that tantrums are necessary, and thus, we shouldn't aim to eliminate them from our and our child's lives completely. The goal of parenting isn't to find every possible way to prevent our child from expressing dissatisfaction, but rather to understand what's happening inside them at that moment. This understanding will guide us in helping them manage their emotions. Tantrums signal a loss of control, a need for protection, and a necessity to explain what's happening in their head because they can't grasp it and are confused by everything happening around them.

Entering our child's mind for better understanding

On the next page is a compelling text from an American mom, Dejah, shared on social media. I've adapted it for smoother reading before sharing it myself.

The enthusiasm from readers each time I share this text surprises me. It's because it helps us precisely understand what's happening in the mind, body, and heart of our two-year-old during this complex period. The purpose of this text isn't to guilt-trip parents but to offer an empathetic view of the toddler. This text helps us better understand and accept our child's behavior, anticipate it, and develop mutual empathy. I'm fully aware that we can't always consider our children's feelings at every moment of our lives, but I believe having a holistic approach is essential.

I'm 2 Years Old

Today, I woke up wanting to dress myself, but I was told, "*No, we don't have time, let me do it!*"

That made me sad.

I wanted to eat breakfast by myself, but I was told, "*No, you'll make too much mess, we don't have time!*"

That frustrated me.

I wanted to walk to the car and get in by myself, but I was told, "*You might fall, come into my arms!*"

That made me cry.

At daycare, when I wanted to play with the blocks, I was told:

"*No, don't just take them for yourself, you need to share.*"

I was angry.

I wanted a hug, but I was told, "*Stop crying, it's okay, it's nothing, go play.*"

I hear a lot of words, but often I don't understand what's being asked of me.

I get scared and don't move.

I lie on the ground and cry.

"*Here, drink this!*"

"*Let me do it, you're too small!*"

"*You're going to spill everything!*"

"Come on, hurry up and finish!"

"Stop your fussing!"...

People talk about fussing, but I feel things inside, it's overwhelming!

No one considers how I feel.

I'm tired and need comforting because I don't control anything.

The things that interest and intrigue me, that my body wants to try, I'm not allowed to do!

How am I to know something will break if I throw it since I DON'T know these things?

How am I supposed to understand *"sharing,"* *"listening,"* or *"waiting a minute"* when I can barely speak?

Don't ask me to sit still quietly!

Don't tell me I'm *"terrible"*!

I'm nervous, stressed, overwhelmed, and confused.

I often need a hug.

I'm 2, 2 and a half, 3 years old...

Listen to me and teach me how to grow.

Our role during a tantrum

As you probably know, a child's brain won't reach its full potential until adulthood. In the meantime, it undergoes numerous developmental stages that will gradually enable it to regulate emotions, at least to the extent it's capable. In a child's early years, it falls upon us, the adults, to regulate their nervous system. Simplistically, imagine the brain as having two parts: an emotional part called the "right brain" and a rational part named the "left brain." During a tantrum, it's the emotional brain that takes over and becomes uncontrollable. The rational brain isn't yet connected to it and can't help the child calm down. The orbitofrontal cortex, the part of the prefrontal cortex that controls our emotions and impulses, doesn't start maturing until between the ages of five and seven.

During a tantrum, the adult acts as a buffer, helping the child regulate their emotion, take a breath, and calm down to move on. If we have the ability, indeed the duty, to play this role for our child, we can only do so under one condition:

having mastered our own emotions beforehand. If we witness two friends arguing violently, we can't calm them down or intervene if we're also in a state of advanced anger. The same applies when our child is experiencing a strong emotion, such as anger in a given situation. If we haven't taken a moment to step back, we won't be able to calm our child. There are many ways to temper our adult emotions daily, and though we've discussed this before, here are some additional strategies:

- Breathing is the best way to disconnect from a strong emotion; simply feel your breath while closing your eyes for a few minutes.
- Meditate when possible,
- Practice heart coherence,
- Exercise regularly,
- Engage in activities that bring you joy,
- Talk to a close friend,
- Write in a journal or record voice notes for yourself...

If managing your emotions seems too complicated, don't hesitate to seek help from a professional. Just as we're advised to put on our own oxygen mask first in an airplane emergency, we must first master our emotions before helping our child temper theirs. This is crucial.

There are experts and then there are "experts"...

We've already explained that an environment where the child feels sufficiently free will help reduce the number of tantrums. Therefore, it's not about teaching them frustration, as many "experts" still advise, despite advancements in neuroscience proving otherwise. "*He's testing you, put him in the corner, or he'll get the upper hand! Show him who's boss!*" is still advice given by experts on young children. This approach, encouraging parents to establish a strict hierarchy with their child as if to prove dominance, is not only unnecessary but shows how much our intuition is worth more than "expert" reasoning that has clearly lost touch with theirs. We don't punish a child, simply because they are in a phase of experimentation, just as a boss doesn't exclude a new intern who messes up the files during their first days of work. Even less should we punish a two-year-old who, as we've seen multiple times, has so little control over their actions.

Unfortunately, these assured directives to parents often leave them feeling helpless. They feel compelled to escalate because they see their child's behavior as disobedience rather than understanding the transformational process happening within them. I assure you that through advanced forms of communication, like what I propose in each chapter of this book, our child will very well understand the limits they shouldn't cross.

What's important isn't the tantrum, but how we handle it.

Let's get into the specifics of managing a tantrum as effectively as possible. If your child expresses their emotion excessively through words, sounds, or gestures, my first advice is to establish physical contact with them. You could touch their shoulders, face, or hug them, showing that you're there for them. The next step is to help the child move on, to create a shock so their brain disconnects from the strong emotion. It's crucial, of course, to revisit the causes of the tantrum, but only later, once calm has returned. For now, the signals are on red, and we need to divert their attention to something else. This technique can calm the child almost instantaneously.

To divert attention, here are several examples:

- Find an object in our bag and show the child how it's used: "*See this pen? It's special because it has four colors. Shall I show you?*"

- Show them a funny picture that you have on your phone.
- Make a quick drawing on a piece of paper, saying, "*Let's draw that little bird on the branch over there!*"
- Point to something around them, for example, "Look, the clouds look like a big cotton candy today, don't you think?"

At this age, it's very easy to divert their attention, so be creative! The more you practice this exercise, the simpler and more natural it will feel. I emphasize again that diversion should absolutely be followed by a phase of verbalizing the situation and the emotion experienced once calm has returned. This ensures we don't overlook the initial situation. More ideas for calming your child during difficult moments are on the next page.

Managing emotions

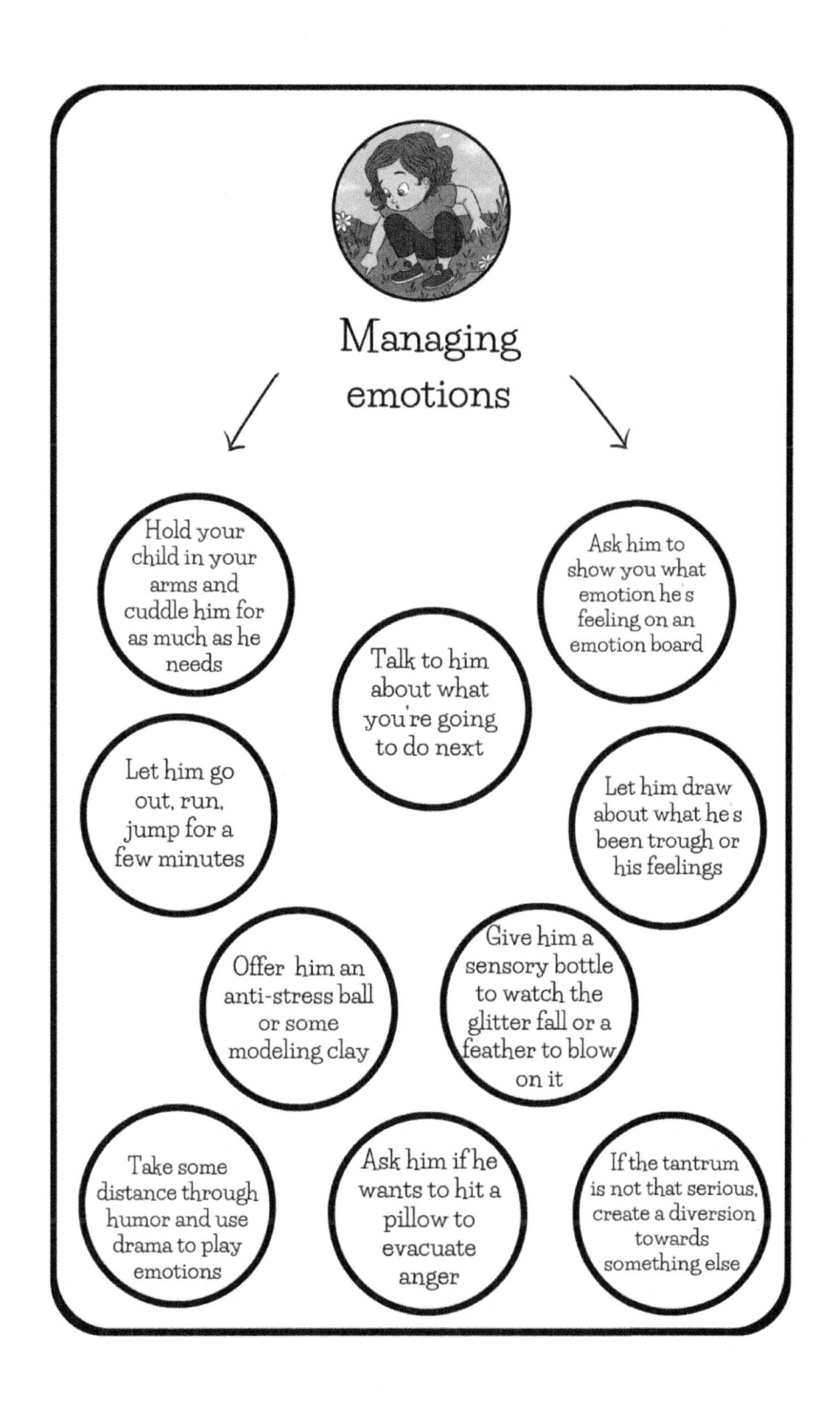

- Hold your child in your arms and cuddle him for as much as he needs
- Let him go out, run, jump for a few minutes
- Talk to him about what you're going to do next
- Ask him to show you what emotion he's feeling on an emotion board
- Let him draw about what he's been trough or his feelings
- Offer him an anti-stress ball or some modeling clay
- Give him a sensory bottle to watch the glitter fall or a feather to blow on it
- Take some distance through humor and use drama to play emotions
- Ask him if he wants to hit a pillow to evacuate anger
- If the tantrum is not that serious, create a diversion towards something else

Identifying emotions

Recognizing and naming emotions is a key step. It involves putting into words what a child is experiencing, in a way they can understand. For example, comforting your child by acknowledging, "*I see you're really upset because that kid pushed you. It's totally understandable to feel that way,*" can be incredibly validating. By identifying and validating their feelings, such as saying,

"*I can see you're angry,*"

"*It makes sense you're sad,*" or

"*Of course, you're excited,*"

we not only acknowledge their right to feel these emotions but also help them recognize these feelings for future reference. This validation teaches them that it's okay to have these emotions, reassuring them that they won't be in trouble for feeling a certain way.

Reflecting after calming down

Once the child has calmed down, it's beneficial to revisit the incident with them at a more peaceful time, not immediately after the event but soon enough so it's still relevant. For instance, during a calm moment like bath time, you could gently discuss the incident, "*Remember when you were playing and that child snatched your toy? That really upset you, and you cried. It's okay to feel upset about that.*" Discussing the incident calmly and at a distance in time helps them process their emotions and understand that it's normal to have such reactions.

A relatable example

A classic scenario that many parents can relate to is the challenge of grocery shopping with children. Supermarkets can be particularly tricky as children often want to buy or touch everything, a desire we might not always anticipate. Instead of explaining why this isn't possible, we sometimes expect them to perform the Herculean task of controlling their impulses. However, in the sensory overload of a supermarket—bright lights, loud noises, and crowds—children find it difficult to manage their desires. Ideally, avoiding bringing a toddler to the supermarket would prevent this issue. If that's not possible, opting for quicker shopping trips to reduce sensory overload can help. We can also prepare them by explaining we're not there to buy toys but can involve them in the shopping process by giving them a small list with pictures of items to collect. Engaging their attention in other ways can also be beneficial:

- Placing them in the shopping cart and asking them to help by moving items from one end to the other,
- Handing them fruits and vegetables to place in a bag,
- Offering a long biscuit to snack on (which you'll pay for, of course),
- Providing headphones with soothing music,
- Giving them coloring books or activities to do in the cart.

However, if the trip is lengthy and your child becomes restless, buying them a small item they ask for might be a reasonable compromise. Expecting a child to resist temptation for an extended period is unrealistic and unfair.

Talking about emotions

There are many resources available to help discuss emotions with children. Books or movies, like Disney's

Inside Out, which is also available as a book, are great because each character represents one of the five basic emotions, easily identified by specific colors (yellow for joy, green for disgust, red for anger, purple for fear, and blue for sadness). This visual cue can be very engaging for children. My children and I have found it helpful to act out the emotions depicted by the characters, associating each with a specific word or sound and exaggerating the facial expressions to match.

— Saying "Yay!" for joy,

— "Ew!" for disgust,

— Shouting loudly for anger,

— Using a trembling voice for fear,

— And pretending to cry for sadness.

Using dramatization, miming, and exaggeration are effective ways to help children understand and express the range of emotions they experience. Sharing our own emotions, no matter how minor, can also teach them that everyone has feelings. "*Wow, I was really frustrated today because I was running late, and it made me grumpy all day.*"

Lastly, many tantrums can be avoided when we don't sweat the small stuff. If your child puts their elbows on the table, it's not the end of the world. If they don't use their fork for a few minutes, let it be. If they spill a little food, it's easy to clean up. Avoiding unnecessary tension is key. When your child makes a mistake or takes their time, show them trust and allow them to do things on their own without scolding. Encouraging them as they navigate their clumsiness or slowness can significantly improve daily life and the overall mood at home. Remember, it's not about the tantrum itself, but how you handle it.

Navigating life's changes

When a new sibling arrives, work becomes more demanding, or it's time to start daycare, the family dynamic can shift. Maintaining the bond with your child is essential, and explaining changes in an age-appropriate manner can help them understand. Beyond words, children are attuned to body language and unspoken feelings from birth. If you're struggling with a situation, or if your child is having a tough time, it's important to talk about it, acknowledge their emotions, and validate them as soon as possible.

"If you know mommy is going back to work soon, I won't be home as much. But we'll still see each other in the morning, at night before bed, and on days off from daycare. It'll be hard for me because I'll miss you a lot, but I'm also looking forward to working again. And I know your nanny will take great care of you. You might feel sad at first, but we'll still spend lots of quality time together!"

This conversation can be repeated and adapted as needed, allowing every family member to express and understand their emotions. This approach fosters a healthy environment for managing emotions and complex situations, ensuring mutual respect and understanding within the family.

If your child hits or bites

We have talked a lot about it; it often happens that our little ones are not able to express their frustration. They may then use a form of aggression towards others. They start biting us, hitting the little brother or the little friend at the daycare without any apparent reason. Let's keep in mind that our child is not trying to be mean or to hurt others. These behaviors simply express an overflow, an emotion, or an unmanaged feeling. Also, it is appropriate not to give in to our first impulse to scold or punish them. This would make no sense to them nor have any impact in the long term.

What I advise to do in case the child hits or bites, is first and foremost to stop the child's action immediately and physically. If he is hitting, we will firmly grab his hand, without hurting him, of course, and tell him: "*No, no, no, we do not hit others, it hurts!* ".

This little tune of "*No, no, no!* " will undoubtedly remind you of other passages in this book. I indeed think that using the same expressions and tones has more impact in the long term. We won't need to yell at our child when stopping his action (the hand that hits or even the face that moves forward to bite), but we will look him in the eyes and express things firmly. Furthermore, we will apologize to the child who was bitten or hit, saying that our little one did not mean to hurt them and that it won't happen again.

"*I know he hurt you, he couldn't control himself, I apologize on his behalf. I will talk to him so it doesn't happen again.* "

It is important that our child hears that we legitimize the pain or shock of the other child, as we usually do for him. Through this, we try to foster empathy in him towards others. 'In a calm moment', later and repeatedly, we will talk to our child about what happened.

"*Do you remember when we were at the park, you bit the little boy, and he was very hurt. I know you didn't want to hurt him, but you must not bite others, it's forbidden, do you understand? No, no, no! We do not bite!* "

If we experiment and observe what works best with our child, we will be able to know how to respond to their emotional outbursts, and it will change our lives!

4. ANTICIPATING CHALLENGING TIMES

This final section is dedicated to navigating the transitional moments in a two-year-old's life and the sometimes difficult phases for parents: bedtime, weaning off diapers and pacifiers, managing diet, and screen time.

Goodnight, little ones!

Many parents struggle with getting their children to bed, regardless of their age. However, establishing good bedtime habits early on can significantly reduce bedtime issues later. It's important to remember that a child's sleep needs vary over different stages of their life and are unique compared to their siblings or peers. Generally, a child between eighteen months and three years requires about fourteen hours of sleep daily, including naps. It's advisable to continue naps until at least three years old, as most sleep experts agree that a napping child won't necessarily be more difficult to put to bed at night. I've observed the same with my own children. A midday rest not only gives the brain time to rest and process information but also offers parents a well-deserved break.

Embracing a new routine

As children grow, parents often consider transitioning them to a different bed, feeling that their child is no longer a baby and ready for this change. It's crucial not to project onto our children the notion that sleep is an unnecessary, unenjoyable task, or worse, a punishment. This mindset is key in managing bedtime routines effectively. Threatening bed as a consequence only reinforces the idea that bed is to be avoided at all costs. Instead, sleep should be viewed as a vital need. The bed is for sleeping or resting, not a place for punishment. Offering rest when a child seems tired, without insisting they sleep, allows them to decide when they need a break, fostering independence and self-awareness.

"I notice you're rubbing your eyes. Would you like to lie down for a bit? You don't have to sleep, but if you feel like it, that's okay. You can come back when you're feeling better, alright?"

This approach has worked well for my children, and even years after the 'Terrific Two' phase, they know when they need a quiet break or an earlier bedtime. Just as we teach them to listen to their hunger cues, we can guide them to recognize their body's need for rest. Explaining our own tiredness and its effects on our mood can also help them make these connections.

Co-sleeping considerations

Deciding whether your child should sleep in their room and bed is a personal choice. Many parents aim for their children to be sleep-independent but send mixed signals. If a child regularly joins you in bed and is always welcomed or even reluctantly allowed, the message is unclear. I've worked with many families who never realized it. If your child gets up every night to join you in bed and you accept this with open arms, or if you grumble, but in the end your child ends the night in your bed, then the message isn't clear.

If you tell your child, "*I'm tired of you sleeping in my bed. I want you back in yours, and I'll help make the transition easier,*" and then follow through with your actions, your child might resist initially but will eventually understand your expectations—that they sleep in their own bed. Conversely, if you instruct them to go to their bed but fail to enforce this, or if you don't articulate your expectations at all, your child might interpret this mixed messaging as:

"*I'm tired of you sleeping in my bed, but also, I like having you close. I'm too exhausted to deal with this, so you might as well keep doing it.*"

This sends a confusing message and could create a complex dynamic. As we've discussed regarding setting boundaries, our children thrive on clarity; ambiguous messages leave too much room for interpretation. In the best-case scenario, they might guess correctly, but more often than not, they'll see our inconsistencies as loopholes. If you enjoy your child's early years and choose co-sleeping—sharing your bed with your child or placing their bed next to yours—that's entirely acceptable.

However, this should be a deliberate choice, not something you fall into out of necessity. It should also be a decision made together with your partner, not just by one parent. I've noticed that sometimes one or both parents may not want to sleep with their child, but because they're unsure how to reverse the situation, their mental health, relationship, and bond with their child suffer. Make decisions based on what you genuinely want, as all parenting choices are valid—except for violence, of course—but be prepared to address any potential issues.

Our decisions can be changed

If co-sleeping seemed like a good idea initially but became too challenging, remember, you only need to answer to your family. The wellbeing of your family is paramount. Consistently allowing a child into the parents' bed or sleeping with them every night is not an ideal solution. Therefore, it's essential to establish boundaries for our own well-being, and doing so doesn't make us bad parents. On the contrary, finding a balance, both individually and as a couple, is crucial. It can take years, especially with the addition of more children. Remember, opinions on this topic are as varied as the people you'll meet, so the decision is yours to make. And the good news is: nothing is set in stone in parenting!

We can adjust our choices based on our family's needs, ideally at a reasonable pace and consistently. Over time, we'll figure out what works best for us and every family member. By setting clear intentions about what we want and don't want, we establish the foundational pillars of our family's values. Many aspects of our children's bedtime routines can seem beyond our control, but being clear about our priorities and the logistical side can simplify things.

Practical tips

If getting your Wonderful Two to sleep is a struggle, consider the advice below and try drafting a detailed bedtime routine. Writing it down can help you visualize the overall plan. Next, sit down with your child during a peaceful moment in the living room to discuss that bedtime has become too challenging and needs to change for everyone's well-being. Even if your child can't express themselves verbally, they'll understand. Be consistent in your explanations, using the same words daily to reinforce their understanding. Then, positively and encouragingly explain the upcoming changes. This family meeting isn't about reprimanding your child for nightly disturbances; it's an opportunity to collectively address and adjust the situation, clearly outlining expectations.

"To start tonight, after our story, we'll share a kiss, and once I leave your room, you're not to get up. Do you understand? Are you allowed to get up after the goodnight kiss? No, no, no!"

Prevent sleep issues

To preempt long-term sleep issues, jot down any bedtime or naptime challenges your child faces. Here's a starter list to customize for your situation:

- The bed,
- The guardrail,
- The number of stuffed animals,
- The nightlight or leaving the door open,
- Room temperature,
- Proximity to a noisy room,
- Sharing the room with another child,
- A room that feels too small,
- Blanket or sleep sack issues,
- Using a pillow or not,
- Bed accessories…

List anything that might disturb your child's sleep, setting the stage for addressing sleep directly. For each listed issue, find an immediate solution. At times, the array of bedtime hurdles can feel overwhelming. Begin with tangible solutions.

Examples:

- Limit your child to one stuffed animal to avoid nightly searches and safety concerns.

- Offer your child a choice between a nightlight or an open door, requiring them to stick with their decision.

You're there to ensure these rules are consistently applied, not to dominate your child but to minimize disruptions when they need calm the most.

If we manage the logistical aspects of bedtime, the child's only focus will be on falling asleep.

The bedtime routine

- You've probably heard the importance of establishing a bedtime routine. It's an effective strategy, adjustable based on family needs or specific periods in the child's life. A bedtime routine is a series of calming steps that prepare the child for sleep. Repeating these actions signals to the brain that it's time for bed. For a child who struggles with time concepts, understanding through repeated actions is easier. If your current routine (or lack thereof) works well, there's no need for change. This means you've found what works for your family.

Consider a bedtime routine lasting around thirty minutes:

- **A moment for hygiene:** bath or shower, depending on your preference. Sometimes, washing our child with a washcloth may suffice. When they're tired, when we're exhausted, lacking patience, or when we'd prefer to spend more time reading a story than managing our child's reluctance to take a bath, this option is worth considering.
- **A moment for dressing:** depending on their ability, we'll dress the child or we'll let them put on two out of five pieces of clothing by themselves. I advise against letting the child choose their clothes at this age (which t-shirt, which pants, etc.). They're too young for that,

it's not a subject of interest for them, and it could lead to pointless power struggles later, especially when you're pressed for time. We often read that giving children choices makes them active participants in their lives, but as with everything, this needs to be nuanced. Considering the fashion preferences of a young child before about five years old is completely artificial. If a child shows opposition to certain clothes or fixation on others, it's likely related to a past experience or something said by someone close to them. In any case, it will pass, so don't think you must only offer them striped t-shirts. Imagine what follows! The child wants to go out in pajamas, and we agree? It's the same with food preferences; they change often, but we don't exclude any food and conversely, we won't always give our child the same thing because they say they only eat pasta. It's up to us to make the distinction. However, the child can certainly take what they need from their wardrobe on their own: pajamas, a pair of socks, etc.

- **A moment for reading:** the child chooses a book, or, depending on the time available, we'll give them a choice between two books that we've selected. We must clearly explain to our child that we'll read only one story and then it's time to sleep. For example, during dinner, we can anticipate by reminding them: "*Later, after the bath, I'll read you a story, do you understand? It's one story, then hug and bedtime, okay?*"

Before reading the story, we'll repeat the same thing. Do not give in to a second story, as this sends a mixed message to your child that could affect future nights.

"Alright, what do I do? I feel bad for not spending more time with the little one! Okay, I'll read another story, it's not a big deal, we'll see tomorrow!"

But since our child isn't capable of being reasonable, because being with mom or dad is too good, they'll likely ask for a third story, if not a glass of water, or their blue teddy bear on top of the wardrobe... Remember, we set clear rules so everyone can have their time—sleep for the child, peace for the parent. Setting rules doesn't make us "a bad parent," but provides the family the opportunity to live together serenely, without the stress of constant confusion. Never punish your child by taking away reading time, at any age; it's an essential connection moment between you!

- **A moment for cuddles:** no need to detail this moment, but I advise against prolonging it or entering into a lengthy discussion with your child. It's a time when the brain should be resting.

If we've anticipated the steps and set a reasonable, approximate time for each, we can, without guilt or fear, turn off the light and leave our toddler's room. If you decide to change things in your ritual based on my advice, note that your child will need a few days to adjust, and you'll need a few days in advance to be ready.

When we're clear and prioritize our child's need for sleep, there's little room for negotiations and multiple requests. What a time saver each evening when bedtime is experienced by all as a step in the day and not as a struggle! It's up to us to control the framework, and if it's clear and fair from the start, we won't have problems later. This is the observation I still make today: no sleep problems with my children.

If your child seems anxious in bed, here are some steps you can take :

- First, consider if their anxiety might be due to a difficult transition they're experiencing, such as the arrival of a new sibling or starting daycare.

- Provide a nightlight or a scarf tied and infused with the parents' scent as an additional comfort object.

- Use a flashlight or even a magnifying glass to search for monsters or other scary creatures together, like detectives. This can help demystify their fears.

- Resist Bringing Them Into Your Bed. Instead, sit on a chair near them for a few minutes. Tell them, "*I'll stay next to you for a bit. Let me know when I can leave.*" Every couple of minutes, ask, "*Is it okay if I leave now?*" This approach gives your child a sense of control, as they're not caught off guard by your departure, which they can't easily gauge the timing of. If this doesn't work, consider trying the more detailed gradual technique mentioned below.

If your child keeps getting up:

Without delay, have a meeting in the living room as described before, and clearly repeat your expectations without endless explanations. Avoid saying things like,

« *You need to sleep because you'll be tired tomorrow, and mom and dad need their time, and...*»

This is not the time for explanations, as it opens the door to negotiations. Your child needs to understand that their actions are disruptive without feeling aggressed. If your child doesn't have any specific issues, has used the bathroom, eaten, etc., they simply need firmer boundaries. Stand your ground and say at their level,

"We agreed you wouldn't get up, remember? Now, do you want to go back to bed by yourself, or should I take you? Which do you prefer?"

If they don't cooperate, put them back in bed—gently, of course, and try to remain emotionally neutral.

Say, "We agreed you wouldn't get up. If you do it again, I'll put you back in bed the same way. Goodnight!"

Repeat this process consistently with the same phrases and actions for every attempt they make to get out of bed. Repeating phrases in the same context helps the brain organize information, which will be true in this situation too. The next day, discuss what happened and reiterate the rules. It might be a bit taxing at first, but after some time, possibly a few days depending on your child, they'll understand that staying in bed is their only option.

It's important to assess your child's behavior at bedtime. Do they need clearer boundaries to help them relax into sleep, or is there a genuine fear or apprehension about bedtime, whether conscious or not? With this understanding, you can tailor your response accordingly.

We don't let the little ones cry

Even when it's challenging to get little ones to bed, it's essential to stay the course. It helps to make these changes as a team or alongside another parent friend who's in the same boat. Encourage each other, celebrate every bit of progress, and try not to dwell on the setbacks. Keep pushing through, and over time, things will fall into place. To stay motivated, keep your eye on the prize: peaceful adult evenings, no bedtime battles, tranquility, and a well-rested child who's less likely to be cranky during the day.

However, even during tough times, it's crucial not to let your child cry it out alone in their bed. Many sleep "experts" suggest letting children cry out their anger to exhaust themselves and eventually fall asleep, claiming it doesn't cause neurological damage. But this approach always circles back to one question: What kind of relationship do we want with our child? It's important to understand the concept of "crying it out" because, of course, children will cry, especially towards the end of the day. It's inevitable and even necessary, but there should be limits.

I briefly tried the method of letting my baby or toddler cry for five minutes, then ten, then fifteen. At the time, I was desperate for solutions to help my first child sleep, despite my many attempts. So, I turned to a "specialist" known for her effective solutions for distressed parents. She confidently shared her miracle method, which, no doubt, has worked for many babies and toddlers... But in these situations, connecting with our intuition is crucial. When we hear our child screaming in despair and we feel deep down that it's wrong, we must listen to our intuition and end the ordeal. It's akin to being told, while our child is having a meltdown, "*Just slap them; it'll calm them down immediately, and they won't do it again!*"

This kind of choice lays the foundation for the type of relationship we want with our child. Later, with my second child, I discovered that gentler solutions exist.

The gradual method

I won't go into detail here, but I'll outline the approach, which could help many parents. The gradual method involves staying with our child until they fall asleep, gradually reducing our presence. This might take a few weeks or months, depending on the child and our endurance. This approach provides the reassurance they need to fall asleep on their own.

- Place your child in bed and sit close by on a chair, placing your hand on them without engaging in conversation. Simply say, "I'll stay with you until you fall asleep. You can rest easy."

- Generally, after twenty minutes, the child will calm down and drift off. Initially, they might be confused by this change and need more time. You can leave once they're deeply asleep, but if they wake up, repeat the process. Ensure you're not distracted by phones or other tasks; your child needs to feel your presence. This can be emotionally taxing, so I recommend that partnered parents support each other and take turns.

- Once the hand-placing step is established, continue to sit near the bed without touching the child until they fall asleep.

- After several days or weeks, you can move the chair a meter away and continue as before.

- When your child seems ready to fall asleep independently, recognizing that you keep your word and are looking out for them, you can proceed to the final step: your child falls asleep alone, and you leave the room immediately.

I hope those who strictly follow this method won't mind my not detailing every aspect. My goal is to highlight the key features of this comforting approach for little ones. Remember, sleep professionals can guide you through this method, which may require psychological support, especially in the beginning. After implementing this approach, I never had sleep issues with my children again. Seeking help for your child's sleep is something I recommend to parents feeling overwhelmed, as lack of sleep quickly impacts our mood and patience. Inquire about the professional's method to ensure a gentle approach that aligns with your values and respects your child. As we've seen, the effectiveness of a method isn't enough on its own.

This age demands our energy constantly, so we can't afford to be drained over an extended period. Addressing sleep issues is a priority for parents of Wonderful Twos, as it significantly improves daily life.

Bedtime checklist

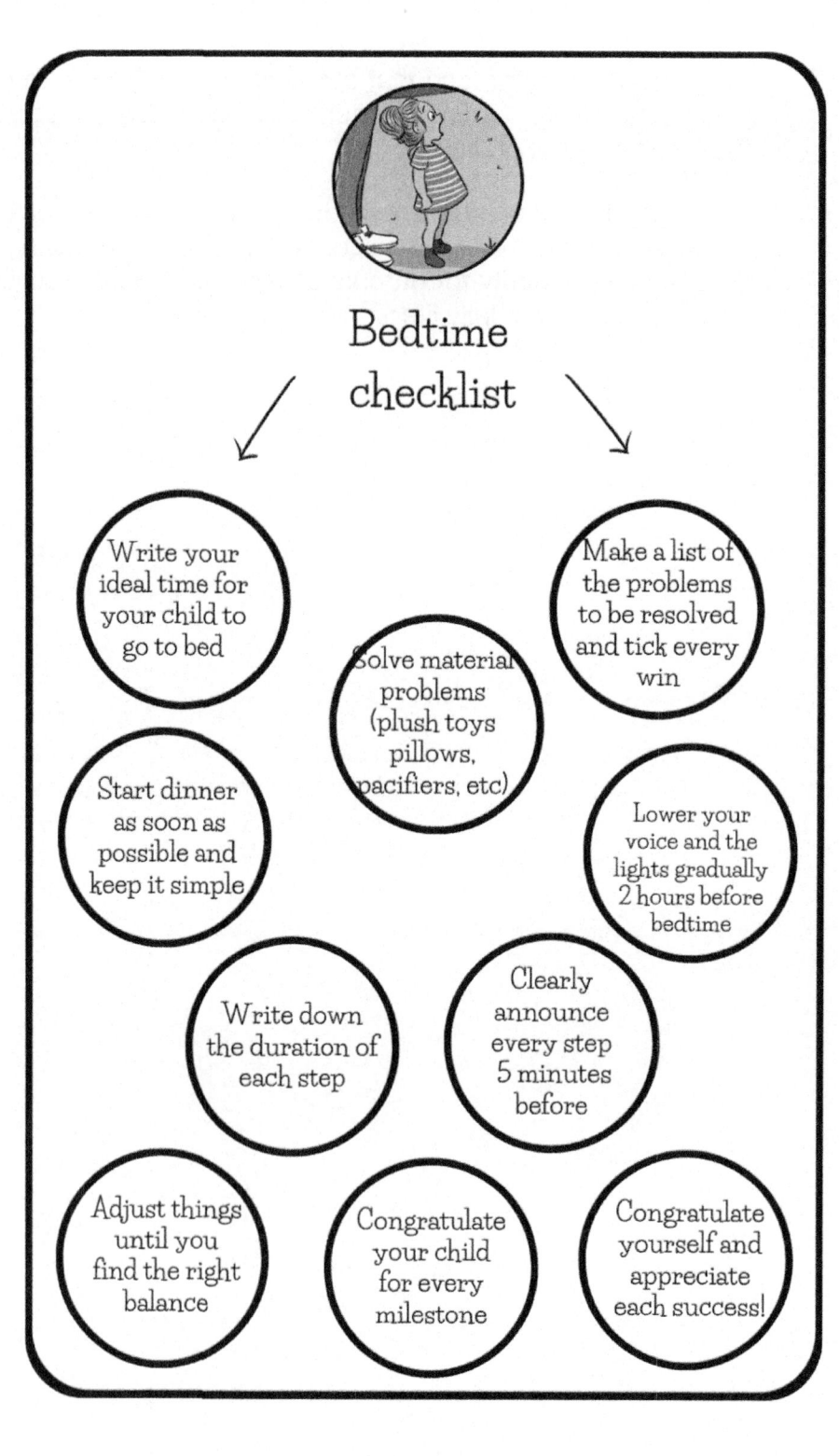

- Write your ideal time for your child to go to bed
- Make a list of the problems to be resolved and tick every win
- Solve material problems (plush toys, pillows, pacifiers, etc)
- Start dinner as soon as possible and keep it simple
- Lower your voice and the lights gradually 2 hours before bedtime
- Write down the duration of each step
- Clearly announce every step 5 minutes before
- Adjust things until you find the right balance
- Congratulate your child for every milestone
- Congratulate yourself and appreciate each success!

Stopping diaper use

There isn't a set age for when children should stop using diapers. Typically, this transition occurs somewhere between eighteen months and three years, but it really depends on a variety of factors. While some parents start the process very early, teaching their infants to signal when they need to use the bathroom, others might use methods that involve preparing the child psychologically for weeks leading up to the day they finally stop wearing diapers. There's a wide range of strategies out there, and I don't believe one is superior to the others. Ultimately, it's about making a choice that suits your family and sticking with it to help your child transition out of diapers and start using the toilet. In this chapter, I won't go into the specifics of the different methods, as I'm not deeply familiar with them and don't have a strong opinion on any in particular. Instead, I'll share some general advice that seems useful for this transition, focusing on a gradual approach, which is the most common way to go about it.

Changing while standing

Once your child is able to stand and balance on their own, I highly recommend changing their diaper in this position. Sit on the floor and change their diaper while they're standing, keeping their hands busy with a toy, for example. This position makes diaper changes easier, preventing your child from wriggling around if they don't want to lie down on the changing table and making it less physically demanding for you. After a few tries, you'll likely find that diaper changes go more quickly and smoothly, and your child will get used to being changed while standing. This method also subtly prepares them for a future without diapers and is especially handy for changes on the go. If you're out and about, your child can lean against a wall for a quick, discreet change. Transitioning to pull-up diapers that mimic underwear can also help during this period. Just like you'd store underwear in your child's dresser, you can keep a supply of pull-ups there and encourage your child to grab one themselves when it's time for a change, fostering their involvement in the process.

It's not a race

Some children will manage to stop wearing diapers after just a few days, while for others, it may take weeks. Our goal is to take things step by step over a long period, not to rush against the clock. When I mention several weeks, I include a period of psychological maturation that the parent must go through before starting what is commonly referred to as "potty training."

It's true that this term can almost seem derogatory, implying that the child is "dirty" before diaper removal, when they simply cannot help it. However, I believe this term can motivate us, especially when we're lacking it, to simply help our child feel more comfortable daily without the discomfort in their lower abdomen. In any case, we must anticipate and not suddenly decide, because it seems like all conditions are met: "*That's it, tomorrow we'll remove the diaper!*" This may be an important indicator that you're ready, but let's not skip steps: preparation is necessary before you start.

Mentally preparing ourselves first

Indeed, there's a significant psychological and logistical phase to consider when we decide to remove our child's diaper. Remember, every child is different, and what worked with your first child may not work with the second. Similarly, methods used by our friends are not a guarantee of success for our child. That's why it's good to think ahead about what might work best for the whole family and stick to it. Also, remember that in our child's life, what we'll remember isn't whether they stopped wearing diapers at two years or two years and nine months. Like the age they started walking, it's a minor detail in their life. The most important thing is that parents are ready and can transmit the right method to their child.

Psychologically, we must be ready for our child to reach this developmental milestone and grow up. During certain phases, as we've seen in the bedtime routine, we sometimes wish our child would stay small and close to us. Unconsciously, we express that we, as parents, still need to take care of their basic needs, and without realizing it, we prevent them from moving on to the next stage. A child who has stopped wearing diapers will no longer need us for going to the toilet, perhaps for wiping at the beginning, but we'll teach them that too soon enough. It's clear that we cannot keep our child in a baby phase simply because we don't want to see them grow up, or because we know this will be our last child. By choosing to raise our children, we promise to be there for them, to meet their needs, and help them grow.

The right timing

If you've just moved, if your child has just changed daycare, if there's been the arrival of another child, or any other new development, don't start yet, wait a few months. Stopping the use of diapers should happen during a stable psychological moment for the child. It will be counterproductive to start this learning and stop after a few weeks without any results. This is because your child is simply focused on the new dynamics of the situation and is trying to manage the changes disrupting their life. They likely won't have the capacity to focus on a new diaper-free routine with all that entails. However, once you decide it's time for your child to stop wearing diapers, don't go back on your decision. Continue for at least two weeks before reviewing and possibly realizing they weren't ready. If you stop too early, it could send a mixed message and potentially delay their potty training by several months.

Family preparation

Deciding that our child will use the toilet like adults, we must be ready for family life to revolve around this topic. It will require a lot of energy, patience, time, and thus, we'll be less available for other things. In any case, I advise going through a period of psychological preparation, first of the parent, as we've discussed, but also of the child and the family. Of course, we'll talk to the child about thinking they're ready to stop wearing diapers, but this could also lead to a small meeting where all family members discuss that the child will soon be diaper-free and that it will require everyone's effort. This might mean, for example, that parents are a bit less available for other children, or that sometimes we might ask one of the older children to assist the little one at times, like staying near the toilet door to reassure them. You'll need to find a balance and start the conversation with the child, without creating too much pressure.

Potty or toilet?

Generally, I don't recommend transitional objects for young children, and I don't recommend using a potty for potty training. Our goal is for the child to adapt to a new space, namely the household toilet and, by extension, those commonly used everywhere. It doesn't seem relevant to get them used to squatting on a potty when they need to be comfortably seated on the toilet. This doesn't seem more cumbersome than a potty, whose system is rather unpleasant, both for the child and the parents, because of the step of transferring waste into the regular toilet. There are toilet seat reducers that can be used to make sitting on the adult toilet more comfortable. There's also the foldable step stool with integrated reducer, which I find particularly practical. Otherwise, you can simply use a step stool to get the child to the right height. For outside the home, a portable reducer might be useful. Take the time to see what's available and also ask for opinions from those around you about these systems.

Is your child ready?

Here are some signs that your child is ready to stop wearing diapers:

- They can climb stairs, indicating their muscles are strong enough for control.
- They stay dry for several hours, especially after naps.
- They can undress themselves at least partially without adult help.
- They let you know when their diaper is dirty (says "pee" or "poop"), or seems bothered by it.
- They show curiosity about the toilet, like books on the subject, visit the bathroom to see, etc.
- They understand simple instructions and can communicate back with words or a nod.

If most of these indicators are present, you can start talking to them about stopping wearing diapers.

What's in it for the child?

Before starting, keep in mind that a young child doesn't really see the benefit of stopping wearing diapers other than the need to be clean or seen as a big kid. Wearing a diaper, not controlling themselves, and being changed by an adult is not only comfortable for them but is also all they've known since birth. Suddenly, we're introducing logistical considerations that aren't of interest to them:

- Interrupting what they're doing to go to the toilet,
- Undressing themselves,
- Dressing themselves,
- Eventually wiping themselves,
- All in view of the whole family,
- Potentially under pressure to perform when asked...

This isn't very motivating for our little one. That's why we'll need to use playful approaches or forms of motivation.

Little rewards

While I don't recommend rewarding our children daily for normal acts (like helping around the house, dressing themselves, etc.), I find it appropriate to offer small gifts during transitional moments like stopping wearing diapers or a pacifier. However, this should be done thoughtfully, not randomly. You'll find all types of charts or motivational systems online for children to use the toilet. Many books also cover the subject. It won't be necessary to buy too many books; one or two will suffice.

You can certainly create your own chart or timeline where you mark with circles the number of times the child goes to the toilet, or if they peed or pooped, with a drawing of a gift at the end. The idea of this type of system is to place a sticker whenever the child goes to the toilet instead of in their diaper. After a certain number of stickers, the child receives a small gift, and if they complete the chart, for example, they receive a larger gift. Of course, the child needs to go to the toilet within a reasonably short time frame, because if the chart spans two weeks, for example, with ten points to earn, it won't really make sense. The chart or timeline should be displayed at the child's height, near the toilet.

I don't recommend imposing this system on external caregivers like nannies, grandparents, or daycare staff. The child will understand the difference and know it's just with their parents that this works. There's no need to create complications for everyone. In any case, the use of a reward chart must be accompanied by motivating, affirming dialogue to help the child understand their progress. Rewards given without showing the child their value are pointless. The child needs to see in our eyes, hear from our mouths that they've succeeded, that they're making progress, that we see it's difficult, but they're increasingly managing to control themselves.

Turning it into a game

Turning it into a game can be both practical and entertaining, like "pretending to sit on the toilet," while fully clothed, for an initial introduction.

"Come, let's sit on the toilet like the grown-ups do. I'll show you how first, then it's your turn, okay?"

The aim is for the child to become accustomed to this new setup and not be deterred by it when they truly need to go.

Additionally, this role-play will prepare the child for the upcoming diaper removal. This can become a game to play at their request, or you might choose to introduce it amidst another activity. Pretend to have an urgent need to pee, using exaggerated expressions, and say, "*Oh no, I really need to pee, please show me where the toilet is! Ah, thank you, but how does this work again? I've forgotten!*"

Another challenging aspect of learning is mastering the ability to pull down their pants and underwear by themselves. Throughout this time, ensure the child only wears joggers or clothes that are easy to remove and put on. During bath time, demonstrate how to pull down and pull up their pants first to their knees, then down to their calves. Soon, we can encourage them to attempt pulling down or up their pants with decreasing assistance until they can do it independently. This could be done before each bath, when removing pajamas, or in the morning, whatever works best for you. Framing this as a game or a routine will make our child more adept at removing their pants when they actually need to use the toilet.

After accomplishing these steps, you'll notice your child is physically prepared, which will save you a lot of time later on, as there will be fewer small tasks to manage. Furthermore, your child will feel more confident, knowing they possess all the skills to go to the toilet alone.

Additional tips

- Don't compel your child to use the toilet on your schedule, but suggest it frequently.
- Express to your child your belief in their ability to know when it's the right time. You might say, "When you feel the urge to pee, let me know! I'll help you get to the toilet."

- During this period, it's inevitable there will be numerous accidents. They might forget they're not wearing a diaper and wet themselves. Though this might stir frustration and impatience in us (which is very understandable), refrain from showing displeasure or disappointment to your child. This only increases their pressure to complete a stage they're still mastering, while their toddler brain is busy processing all sorts of information every moment.
- Also, avoid punishing your child for accidents. Don't ask them to change themselves or clean up; they're too young for that. This would be more humiliating than educational.
- Apart from sharing with a select few if it matters to you, avoid broadcasting every step of your child's potty training journey outside the home. It's a part of their privacy. Nonetheless, you can share significant progress occasionally and without pressure: "You know, it's been a week since he/she has worn a diaper and has been using the toilet!"
- Once training begins, outings with your child might pose a challenge. Plan ahead for bathroom breaks. Carry cleaning supplies, but bringing diapers might lead to regression. Initially, limit outings to places with accessible toilets to simplify the process. If a diaper is necessary, save it for truly complicated situations and avoid mentioning it beforehand. If no other option is available, like being outdoors without access to toilets, let the child relieve themselves discreetly. This is preferable to reverting to diapers, as children can struggle with understanding nuances and exceptions.
- For naps and nighttime, continue using a diaper for your child and phase it out once it remains dry for several consecutive days. Make a distinction between daytime continence, which the child can somewhat control, and nighttime, when they're asleep and not in control of their consciousness or will.

- Nighttime bathroom visits can be more challenging for a child. You might consider waking them to establish a habit of nighttime toilet use, but this could disrupt their sleep pattern. It's up to you to try and see if it fits your situation. Many child psychologists believe that before the age of six, nighttime wetting isn't considered enuresis, and continuing to use diapers at night if they're still wet is advisable. Waking up wet in the morning or in the middle of the night is unpleasant. Explain that wearing a diaper at night is to prevent discomfort but doesn't mean they've regressed to being a baby.

"You're doing great with using the toilet during the day, but at night it's still tough for you because you're deeply asleep and can't feel when you need to pee. We'll keep the diaper on for now, but if you wake up at night and need to pee, you can go to the toilet! We'll remove it later, it's okay, it will happen in time."

In conclusion, I believe as many approaches exist as there are children or child care professionals. Thus, the key, as always, is to align with our chosen approach. Allow yourself the time to implement it, maintain consistency, and focus on the child's advancements rather than their setbacks. Strive to find a balance to guide your child through this significant milestone, sometimes with more tenderness, other times with more encouragement.

Sorry I no longer eat brocoli
My friend Ben says a little tree will grow inside my belly

Removing the pacifier

Moving away from the pacifier marks another significant milestone in a child's life. For various reasons, most parents offer their baby a pacifier from birth, often because it provides real soothing. As the child approaches preschool age, or a bit before, parents often wish for their child to wean off the pacifier, as it no longer serves the same purpose, and the child can do without it. This perspective is supported by numerous health specialists. Moreover, to prevent dental deformation, it's advisable not to let the child use a pacifier too long, roughly beyond three and a half years. Like with diaper removal, the approach can vary: whether to offer a pacifier to the child, at what age to remove it, and by what method are all up to individual choice.

In my view, after the first quarter of entering preschool, children are likely ready to give up their pacifier. Up to about three years old, children are often soothed and calmed by the pacifier. It comforts them and focuses their attention during times of emotional fragility. Starting preschool in September is a significant transition for both the child and the family, making it an inopportune time to take away the pacifier. Typically, children need about a quarter to feel confident in their new environment. That's when we can try, if not done before; keeping in mind, of course, that this is up to the parents who know their child best. Past the age of four or four and a half, it's somewhat troubling to see a child still with a pacifier, given their physical size, no longer baby-like, and their psychological maturity. I align with most specialists who urge parents to help their child move past this stage at this relatively late age. Our role, naturally, involves supporting the child and not rushing the process, yet we cannot wait indefinitely for readiness. As discussed earlier, we cannot keep our child at a stage they've outgrown. If we recognize that they have the emotional maturity to find comfort beyond the pacifier, we'll assist them in making this transition.

You'll find that for some children, giving up the pacifier happens quickly, while for others, it takes more time. Don't worry; everything eventually falls into place. Note that, like with stopping diaper use, a child might not see an immediate benefit in giving up their pacifier. It's a source of comfort, a soothing object, much like a beloved toy, triggering pleasant emotional responses: "*When I use my pacifier, I feel calm, it reminds me of being a baby, and I feel good.*" It's up to us, as parents, to initiate and motivate our child to give it up when we feel ready.

How to proceed?

To prepare your child to stop using the pacifier, you'll find plenty of resources like books or kits with accessories, but they are not necessary. We saw in the chapter on stopping diaper use that visualizing steps on a chart and displaying it can help the child see their progress and be motivated by the fun aspect. The same approach can be applied to the pacifier by creating a simple chart. For example, mark each half-day the child places their pacifier in a designated drawer. Adding small illustrations or a photo of your child can personalize it. Like with the diaper chart, after a certain number of points or stickers, the child receives a gift. You might offer a small gift for a day without the pacifier and a larger one at the end of the week, depending on what feels right to you. The key, as with many things, is to progress gradually.

A challenging phase

Avoid constantly telling the child that pacifiers are for babies because we must remember this is hard for them. It's not just a matter of willpower; it's emotional and psychological. Imagine being told as an adult, "*From now on, you're no longer going to use your smartphone!*" While the idea might be striking, even liberating for some, giving up something we're accustomed to would be very difficult, not just logistically but psychologically as well. Of course, the comparison isn't exactly the same, but the main point is clear: it's not just about willpower, but about habit.

For our little ones, who don't have the emotional resources we do for long-term endurance, the pacifier has been a part of their lives since birth. That's why I emphasize the motivational aspect: a playful approach and a reward system seem relevant in this context.

Removing the pacifier as a family

Gather family members to discuss the idea that the child will start trying to go without the pacifier, and that we will support them. It could be helpful to ask each family member for ideas to compensate for the absence of the pacifier. Explaining to everyone what the child might feel without the pacifier, with concrete examples, will help grasp the stakes and foster empathy towards the little one. The absence of the pacifier will require a lot of comforting through hugs, quality time, games, etc. Sometimes we'll need to distract, draw the child's attention to something else, and engage them more so that gradually the lack of the pacifier is filled.

Fewer pacifiers

Effectively reducing the number of pacifiers the child has will aid the process. For instance, you might ask the child to select only two pacifiers out of their usual ones and to store them in a specific drawer or box when not in use. The idea is to keep them out of sight as much as possible to minimize thought about them. If the child understands the principle of limiting and centralizing pacifier storage, you could suggest choosing just one of the two pacifiers a few days later. Similarly, place it in a designated storage spot.

Motivation through words

Verbalizing progress to the child is crucial. Offer praise, encouragement, and possibly share what you think they might be feeling.

"Wow, I'm so proud of you. It's not easy giving up the pacifier, especially since it's been a comfort since you were a baby. You've shown a lot of courage and determination in giving it up. Do you feel how you're growing up inside?"

Such discussions are vital to continue motivating the child psychologically and providing relevant feedback. As mentioned with stopping diaper use, motivating a child with gifts alone is insufficient. We need to articulate the psychological shifts occurring within them, showing them they're undergoing emotional maturation.

"You don't need a pacifier now because you're big in your heart and mind."

I often use the phrase "big in your mind" with my children to differentiate from "big in size." It helps children understand there are two types of maturation: physical and psychological.

When it becomes too difficult

There will be moments when it's challenging for your child, and you'll be tempted to give them their pacifier because they're crying, asking for it, or you're pained to see them like this. This is perfectly normal. These tough times are necessary, as in many situations throughout life. It's an opportunity to teach our child a valuable lesson for the long term. These are the moments when our child will need us the most to motivate, encourage, and support them like a coach.

"I know this is hard. I understand your pain, I get that it's tough for you. It's okay to cry. I understand you feel like throwing a tantrum, but I know giving you the pacifier now won't solve the problem. It will only make things harder for you later."

It's beneficial to remind the child of the progress they've made, mentioning both their achievements and the challenges they've faced.

"We need to stay strong, and we'll do it together. You've already made a lot of effort, well done! Is there something particular you'd like to do to feel better? Do you need something? A hug? Your favorite toy? Do you want us to do a puzzle together? What would make you happy? What could help you calm down and soothe your anger?"

Taking a step back, we see how guiding our child through difficulties, whether it's stopping the pacifier or diaper use, teaches them invaluable life lessons. We can refer back to these moments during other challenging times they may face.

"Do you remember when you stopped using the pacifier? It was so tough for you at times... But you persevered, you were strong, brave, and then you were proud of yourself."

In my view, this is how we prepare children to better understand themselves and recognize their inner strength. For parents, it might be helpful to plan adult outings, moments for ourselves, to rejuvenate and relieve the emotional tension associated with this significant transition.

Stopping the bottle

Stopping the bottle is somewhat different from stopping the pacifier, mainly because of the dental issues it can cause. Delaying the cessation of bottle use can expose the child's teeth to constant milk acidity, inevitably leading to cavities. It's essential to consider this to avoid the dental problems often observed after three years when the child is still using a bottle. To facilitate the transition, we can plan a shopping trip where the child picks out a bowl for their breakfast cereal. This can motivate them, and they'll likely be proud to pour their milk into their new bowl the next day.

Sippy cups aren't truly necessary, so an adult glass should be offered to the child at meals when they're thirsty. Also, avoid opting for a water bottle or offering a straw as a substitute for sucking, which the child doesn't really need. Drinking isn't supposed to be fun; it's a natural necessity.

Replacing cuddle times

If your child enjoyed cuddling with you in the morning with their bottle or in the evening before falling asleep, you can certainly keep this cuddle time, just without the bottle. To assist in this transition, you might offer a scarf or an item belonging to one of the parents for the child to sleep with. If desired, introduce a new ritual, like reading a book or drawing in a notebook, to replace bottle time and help the child through this transition more effectively. As with the diaper, we'll need to initially find emotional compensations to ease the difficulties related to withdrawal. I want to remind you that when we aim for our child to outgrow the diaper, pacifier, or bottle, it's never about punishing them, mocking them, or rushing through regressions. Doing so would inevitably set the child up for failure. In conclusion, I'm convinced that in all these transition situations, if the parents know what they want, if their goal is to help and guide their child through these phases, things will go as smoothly as possible. Therefore, the most important thing is choosing the right moment when both the parents feel ready and the child is too. Once we begin, we'll find ways to sustain our efforts.

When mealtime becomes a challenge

Around the preschool years, many parents face difficulties getting their child to eat. This often leads to daily frustrations at mealtimes and even at bedtime. Teaching our child to eat is a fundamental part of their upbringing, and I believe many issues can be avoided if addressed early. Like with anything, it's advisable to first take a step back and then tap into our creativity. It's especially important to examine our own relationship with food to avoid projecting our issues onto our child. If, for instance, we often diet or have a complicated relationship with food, eating more sweets or in larger quantities to compensate for unaddressed emotions, we shouldn't pass this on to our child. Conversely, if we're accustomed to eating lightly or the same foods repeatedly, it's also best to keep this to ourselves. Our child should start with a clean slate when it comes to food.

It's crucial not to create pressure during meal times. If your child is currently hesitant about eating, don't obsess over it or discuss it widely, as this could exacerbate the issue. A child's reluctance today might change tomorrow; nothing is set in stone unless we make it so by focusing on it. Instead, let's be proactive and come up with simple and creative ideas to improve our child's relationship with food. The following paragraphs will offer several suggestions. Always remember that eating, nourishing oneself, is a vital function. Thus, a child should not eat just to please us or because they are coerced.

While the playful approaches I share are meant to be sprinkled throughout the child's life, whether there's a food issue or not, they should not become the norm for every meal. Turning each meal into an experiment or a game could be counterproductive. Moreover, we need to find a natural way for the child to eat without resorting to constant tricks, like putting them in front of a screen or playing with them to distract from eating. We're not raising robots but future responsible adults! Instead of focusing on potential mealtime tensions, imagine food as a way to connect with our child, setting aside our urgency for them to eat at all costs. There's a world of tastes, colors, and textures for the child to explore. Children are highly connected to their senses. What could be more natural, creative, and straightforward than leveraging this to help them enjoy the food offered?

Personal note: The meals I prepare are usually very simple and require minimal preparation. I'm not an organized mom who plans meals in advance! I never plan menus or shop accordingly, but this doesn't stop me from providing my children with proper meals daily. I mention this to reassure parents who might feel uninspired in the kitchen. You don't need to constantly innovate or offer elaborate dishes to your children daily. Just as some parents create educational materials for their children or spend a lot of time developing their musical ear, everyone has their style, and that's perfectly fine. Let's do what we can, with love; that's what counts and is enough for our child! If we find time to prepare slow-cooked meals during the week, that's great, but it's not a necessity.

Exploring the kitchen with our child

When you have a quiet moment, go to your kitchen, open the fridge, and look at what's available. Note down any creative ideas that come to mind without overthinking how to use them.

Some examples:

- Spices add color, allow for sprinkling, are fun, and have unique scents.
- Vegetables can be sorted by color or how they're eaten, raw or cooked. They can be peeled with a peeler or simply washed. With lettuce, there's no need to peel, just wash thoroughly and remove the bottom.
- Tomatoes contain juice, whereas bell peppers don't. But both have seeds.
- Cucumbers and zucchinis are similar because they're from the same family. One is eaten cooked, the other raw.
- Fruits are generally liked by children. Some can be peeled with fingers, like oranges, mandarins, and grapefruits, all members of the citrus family.
- Lemons join the list. What do they have in common? Seeds, juice, acidity.

This could continue with all the foods in our cupboards and fridge. The idea, as you've gathered, is to go back to basics because children love explanations, especially when done playfully and hands-on. They enjoy understanding, recognizing flavors, and remembering, for example, that they ate mandarins last time at grandma's. This approach will help them form a pure and healthy connection with food.

Cooking with our child

Inviting our children to participate in meal preparation from as young as two years old is a delightful way to foster their enjoyment of meals. We can introduce them early to washing foods, handling them, and cutting simple items. By three years, a child can help prepare a fruit salad with bananas and strawberries, for example. Cooking is not only enjoyable for children but also a way to grow their appreciation for a wider range of foods as they become familiar with different textures, smells, and unique properties. Occasionally, we can allow our children to eat with their fingers, especially before two and a half years, but we should always offer utensils suited to their hand size as soon as possible:

- A glass made of glass, metal, or melamine,
- Metal utensils, possibly with melamine handles,
- A small knife for easily cutting foods like cooked potatoes or bananas,
- A simple plate,
- A large fabric bib or a napkin around the neck for wiping.

It's crucial not to get overly upset when our child makes a mess. They will soon learn the proper way to eat. Be patient, it will come, and don't hesitate to show them how regularly. Remember, eating neatly is a learned skill that requires time, mess, and, consequently, our patience.

Fun utensils

Adding a bit of whimsy to meals can make them more enjoyable for children. Why not occasionally serve food on creatively decorated plates? Semolina can become beach sand, a yolk the sun, and carrot sticks its rays... I've often used various containers and accessories to make mealtime fun for my children, even when there were no particular issues with food. My goal was simply to delight them. For instance, I've used small storage boxes shaped like hearts or little picks for eating. Seeing their eyes light up because I placed a panda-shaped pick on top of a strawberry instead of its stem is priceless! Skewers can be used for fruit or chicken and crunchy vegetable kebabs. Presenting meals this way changes everything for a child, making it much more fun!

Teaching hunger management

From two years old, your child can begin serving themselves from a dish. Offer them a large salad bowl or the day's food with a big spoon and encourage them, "*Here, you can serve yourself.*" They'll enjoy filling their plate and may even serve themselves again. It's okay if they initially take too much or too often. We'll teach them to gauge portion sizes over time.

"*Today, try to take only what you'll eat without leaving anything at the end. It's better to serve yourself small amounts multiple times rather than having a plate too full that you won't finish. Do you understand? Go ahead, serve yourself.*"

By progressing gradually, the child learns what's expected and how to manage on their own. You'll notice that in the ideas I suggest, I aim to divert attention away from the "content" of the meal. It's a pleasant diversion that allows the family to relax and enjoy a nice, shared moment. This means the child may forget their dislike for certain foods in favor of the enjoyable time spent. For foods the child seems not to like, we'll offer them regularly in different forms, allowing the child to gradually incorporate them into their diet: zucchini in fritters, mixed into mashed potatoes, in savory waffles, etc.

At the end of the meal, it's beneficial to tell our child what was in the dish they just enjoyed.

"Did you know what you ate tonight? The fish balls you liked? Well, they had zucchini in them. Remember last time you didn't like zucchini much? When I put it in the fish balls, you enjoyed it! Isn't that great?"

Even if your child is young, they'll understand and perhaps be more open to trying zucchini in a less disguised form next time:

"Remember, last time, we had zucchini in the fish balls. It was good, right? How about we try it in a different way?"

This approach allows you to reintroduce zucchini into your child's diet. Remember, tastes evolve over time, even for adults. Weren't there foods you disliked years ago that you've come to enjoy? The same goes for our children, who go through phases, albeit shorter ones. Therefore, and reassuringly, there's no inevitability. We often complicate life over food or any issue our child faces for a period. In reality, often all it takes is a step back and the use of playful, creative approaches to completely change the atmosphere at home.

There's nothing more delightful than adding a touch of whimsy and "magic" to daily life. For me, this is not just an extra; it's essential and often what helps me overlook the logistical nightmare! We don't need to wait for our children to have food issues to try all this. Our children are so receptive to surprises, they appreciate our efforts, and this creates a lot of lightness in everyday life. Fantasy enhances every situation, primarily for the joy of sharing, and in the context of food, it helps establish healthy family eating habits.

Themed meals

To conclude this chapter, here are some themed meal ideas that can add a little variety to the daily routine. Use them as often as you like, especially when you want to break the monotony or when your child is having difficulties with food. Of course, the aim isn't to turn family life into a continuous party, but these ideas should keep you inspired for years!

- Pizza Night: Prepare it with your child, allowing them to choose and place their toppings.
- Chef's Evening: Family members form teams, and the child rates the dishes with hearts, for example.
- Finger Food Feas: Corn on the cob, cherry tomatoes, mini sausages... perfect for hands-on eating.
- Picnic Style: Lay a blanket on the floor, pretend you're in the forest. "I hope that big squirrel doesn't come for our chips!"
- Buffets: Children love them because they offer a wide selection and the chance to serve themselves. Present appetizers and main courses simultaneously for variety.
- Chromatic Meals: "Today, we're only eating white foods for lunch, any ideas?" (eggs, cauliflower, rice...).
- Crepe Day: Both savory and sweet. Electric crepe makers are very handy for this.
- Pie and Tart Day: Use puff pastry and leftovers from the fridge to create something delicious.
- Creative Plates: Each person prepares a fun plate for another family member.
- Favorite Meal: Composed of each family member's favorite dish, decided in advance. The child picks their favorite main course, a parent chooses the appetizer, etc.

- Surprise Meal: Prepare a unique meal with your child for the other parent without telling them.

These varied approaches offer numerous ways to engage children with food through playful yet natural means. They're opportunities to preempt problems and enjoy delightful family moments.

Creative meal ideas

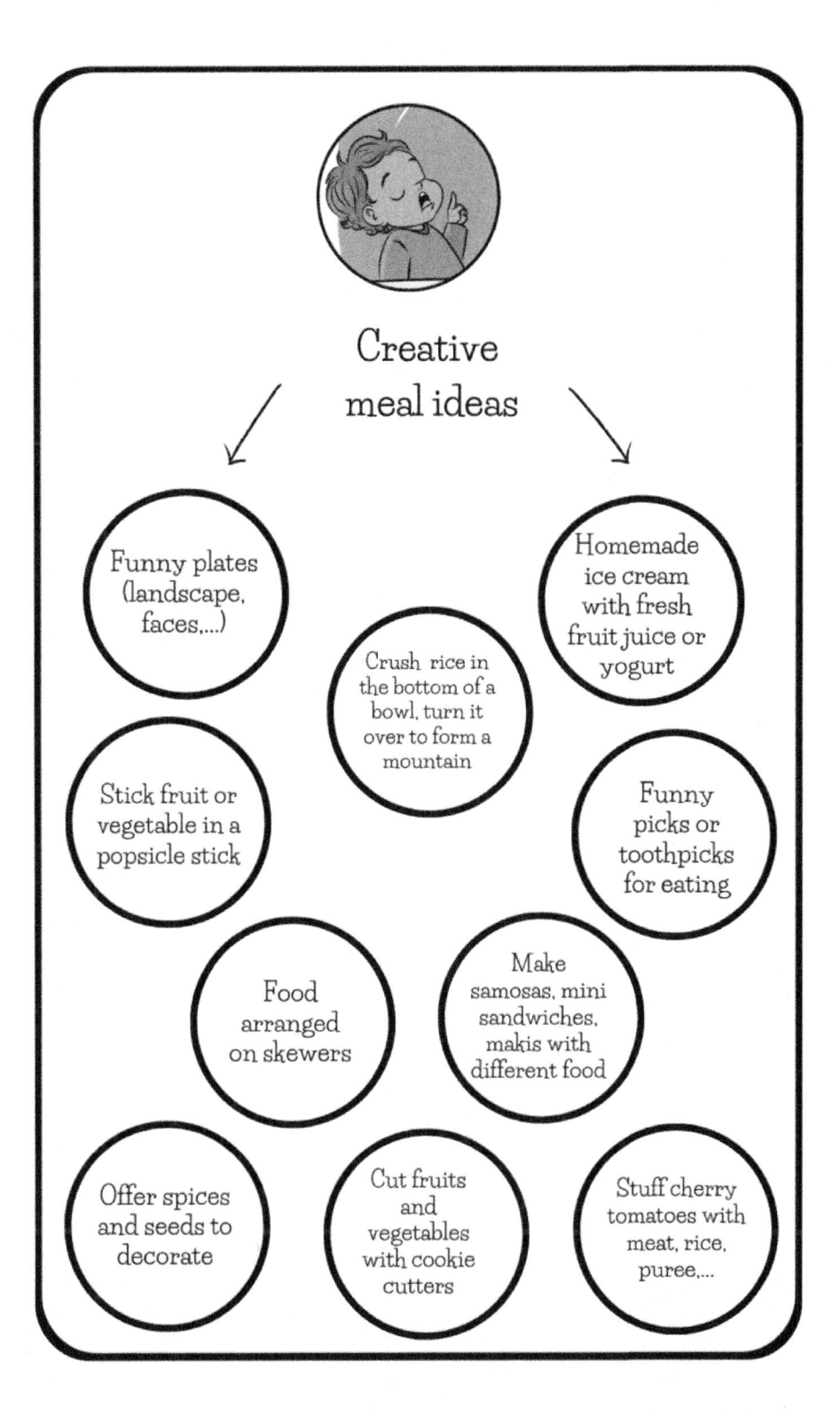

- Funny plates (landscape, faces,...)
- Stick fruit or vegetable in a popsicle stick
- Crush rice in the bottom of a bowl, turn it over to form a mountain
- Homemade ice cream with fresh fruit juice or yogurt
- Funny picks or toothpicks for eating
- Food arranged on skewers
- Make samosas, mini sandwiches, makis with different food
- Offer spices and seeds to decorate
- Cut fruits and vegetables with cookie cutters
- Stuff cherry tomatoes with meat, rice, puree,...

Navigating screen time for little ones

The final critical issue I've chosen to delve into, due to its prominence in the lives of our youngsters, revolves around screen time. It's a fact: children are being introduced to screens increasingly early, often before reaching the age of three. This matter deeply resonates with me, as I believe the digital omnipresence and proliferation of screens in our society are reshaping family dynamics and behaviors. Parents today often feel overwhelmed, guilty, or at a loss amidst the sea of advice and directives regarding screen usage.

Through my own research and observations concerning children's interaction with screens, a consensus among professionals suggests that children under three years old should ideally not be exposed to screens. This recommendation aligns with the understanding of their developing brains, which absorb information without the capacity for adequate processing. Furthermore, young children need to engage actively with their environment to hone their physical skills and gain a comprehensive understanding of the world around them.

Rest assured, children under three years do not need screens, and this stance extends beyond that age. While some argue that screens offer enrichment by exposing children to moving animals or cultural experiences from other countries, I firmly believe that screens are not essential for a child's brain development or intelligence. They are merely tools at our disposal, but by no means a necessity.

We're discussing a world where screens are increasingly prevalent in children's lives, so let's not kid ourselves; we know many children under three have access to screens. Thus, advising parents simply not to expose their children to screens before three years isn't practical. We must consider the reality of families, especially those with multiple children, where it's impossible to avoid screens entirely when the older child uses them in the living room. Moreover, since programs are marketed to toddlers, this encourages parents to legitimize screen time and meet a need for peace and quiet.

It's crucial to remember that screens should never be used as a primary form of childcare to free up time for ourselves. A child grows through interaction, not passivity. And while it may be tempting, this should not become a habitual family lifestyle. Screen time should also not be used as a bargaining chip for "good behavior" or as a constant threat to ensure compliance. Such practices not only manipulate psychologically and create power struggles but also introduce an unhealthy relationship between the child and the parent, with an object as the medium of pressure. Parental authority should stand on its own without resorting to external crutches like screens or sweets. The less we rely on these tactics, the smoother and more reasonable will be our long-term communication about screen time.

The perils of screen omnipresence

Screens have become a source of significant and nearly irreversible issues within families:

- Attention difficulties,
- Sleep problems,
- Academic challenges,
- Disconnection from reality,
- Loss of physical activity in favor of sedentary lifestyles,
- Social interaction impacts...

These are among the negative effects observed not just in teenagers but increasingly in younger children. As children grow, screens contribute to complex dynamics with parents. It's vital for parents of young children to be aware of this now, while they still have control over screen exposure.

Embracing a thoughtful approach

The simplest way to coexist with screens is by not making them a focal point. Similar to our discussion on food, unnecessary tension or endless bargaining should be avoided.

"Just one more episode, please?
— Alright, but only one.
— No, two, please, just two."

If we allow such negotiations at two years old, they quickly become unmanageable. A clear, thoughtful approach helps us stand firm.

Prioritizing content

What significantly impacts our child's behavior is not so much the amount of screen time but the content they consume. With the decline in program quality amid a surge of unlimited offerings, content creators compete by producing more to consume, leading to a dilution of quality. Modern cartoons are churned out en masse, catering to quantity demands rather than quality.

Consequently, merchandise and advertising related to these shows infiltrate our lives, swiftly transforming our two-year-olds from children to consumers, almost with our tacit approval. The allure of unlimited content may lead our children to demand the latest character from a cartoon touted as educational, promising to teach basic vocabulary, colors, and numbers.

Having scrutinized the production and content of such cartoons, I can assert they offer no educational value. They lack artistic effort and fail to engage children's imagination or thought processes. Despite being marketed as "educational," these programs entice parents seeking guilt-free screen time.

"Our child is learning while watching!"

Children become accustomed to low-quality imagery and narratives, making it harder to limit screen time later. A well-designed picture book or toy will teach them more while engaging their imagination.

We must sift through available content before limiting screen time. It's our responsibility to select for our children based on quality, not their preferences or what content providers promote. Taking time to preview a few episodes of a show is crucial. Comparing older cartoons to new ones reveals a stark difference in ambiance. In 3D animations, the harsh color contrasts fail to create warmth or beauty. Characters are often exaggerated, straying far from reality.

This calls for smart moderation, as a bit of fantasy can benefit, but our children should not be receptacles for every trend. This is especially true for young children's brains, which can't differentiate between reality and fiction, having limited experience with the real world. Fortunately, many animations and films are far superior to those mentioned. Revisiting cartoons from your childhood might offer better alternatives. My approach may seem strict, but I'm convinced these details contribute to creating a positive environment for children's development.

Managing screen time

Once you've vetted what your children can watch, the next step isn't to let them view whatever they want, whenever they want, just because the content has been filtered. It's crucial to remain vigilant in our homes and not to delegate the responsibility of screen time to our children, just as with the selection of content. It falls upon us, as parents, to take charge and establish clear guidelines for screen use. Like with many aspects of raising our children, a balanced approach is necessary. We shouldn't let our children in front of screens all day, but we also shouldn't overreact if we catch them engrossed in a cartoon at their aunt's house. I believe that a limited screen time of about twenty minutes per day doesn't harm a child's brain development before the age of three. Of course, avoiding screen time entirely is preferable, but if you occasionally need a brief break, it's a viable option. If screen time extends beyond that, it's better to opt for short viewing periods with regular breaks so their brain can process what they've seen.

Additionally, engaging with your child about what they've watched can help reduce passivity. Tailor your questions to their language level, with simple yes or no answers or more detailed responses. You might ask if they remember the characters' names, if they can recount the story, what they liked most about the episode, or if anything scared them. Understanding the importance of moderate screen use and maintaining control over both the duration and content of what your child watches will help you find a sustainable balance for everyone.

I didn't know grown ups also needed training wheels!

TO CONCLUDE

Reflecting on the early years of my children to distill the best of those times has been a magical experience. The age of two stands out as particularly special, presenting us with a pivotal choice: do we resist their impulses, curiosity, and clumsiness, or do we embrace a more complex approach that aligns more closely with our educational philosophy?

Terrible Two or Wonderful Two?

Of course, actively striving to understand our little ones and finding respectful solutions initially poses more of a challenge. Unlearning past reflexes, curbing our immediate reactions, patience, controlling our urge to dominate, or simply our instinct to shout represents a significant challenge! Like all parents, we'll make mistakes, feel inadequate, powerless, weary, and exhausted at times. And like all children, ours will still throw tantrums, and we won't always succeed in connecting with them.

But here's the good news: this too shall pass!

During this period, we'll learn so much! Firstly about our child, but also about ourselves, our emotion management, our ability to push our limits, to decode our child, to foster new aspects of their personality, to navigate difficult moments together, and more.

Don't we then hold keys that will serve us for life? That's certainly what I felt as my children grew. While my teaching career provided me with specific educational skills, I had never been so closely involved with toddlers over such an extended period. Later, the conscious and proactive approach I experimented with my children from an early age evolved into various educational methods I now use to advise families.

Today, most parents seem proud to align with one camp, be it traditional methods or the "positive education" movement. Unfortunately, this lacks nuance, creating discomfort in society, with each side believing their approach is superior. My observation is that no single educational approach can precisely meet the needs of both the child and their parents. We can thrive in a pluralistic approach. Let's not forget our society is undergoing a transition with working mothers not just fathers, single-parent families, blended families, etc. Although children remain the same, our lifestyles have changed, neuroscience has advanced, and we need to consider various factors. Adhering strictly to old models or, conversely, to very recent ones and picking sides seems perilous. Beyond dividing parents, it risks leading each astray.

In my view, the best education stems from our intuition, not rigid but clear in its broad strokes. It considers both our child's needs and our own. That's why nuanced education is so crucial! Building confidence in our parenting role takes time. Walking this path hand in hand with a little companion who will never judge us and always be willing to follow makes the journey all the more beautiful. Children possess a purity that connects us to truth and depth in a world that seems to steer us away from these values. Perhaps that's why I'm so devoted to them and to preserving their innocence as long as possible.

This book is deeply personal to me, from the illustrations to anecdotes about my children and my professional experiences with my students. I aimed to maintain my authenticity and convey my message as an expert while allowing my sensitivity free rein. A little confession: that surge of curiosity, the need to understand everything, the connection to fantasy, and that characteristic impatience of the Wonderful Two also mirror my adult personality!

I hope this book inspires you to spread the term "Wonderful Two®"!

My journey

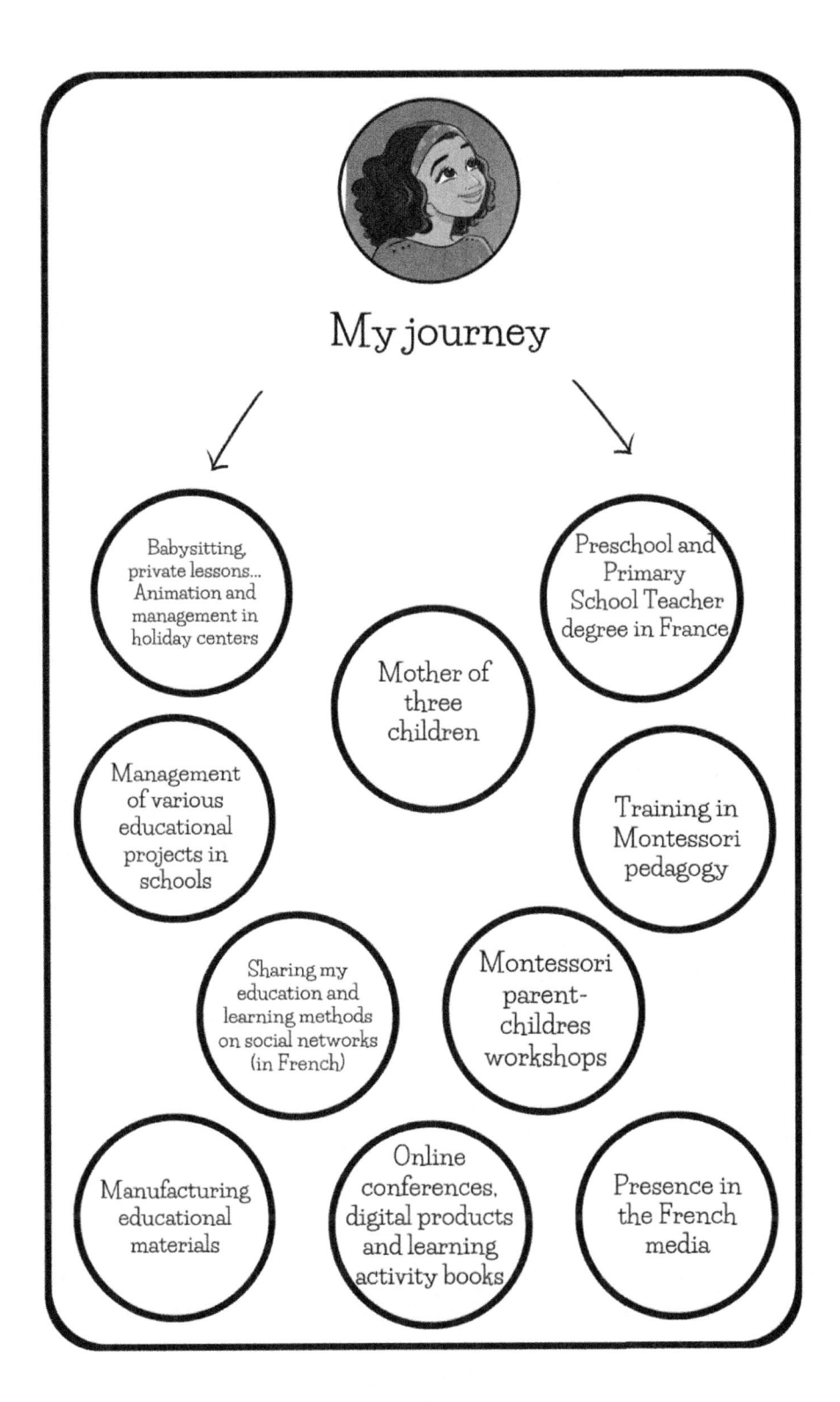

- Babysitting, private lessons... Animation and management in holiday centers
- Preschool and Primary School Teacher degree in France
- Mother of three children
- Management of various educational projects in schools
- Training in Montessori pedagogy
- Sharing my education and learning methods on social networks (in French)
- Montessori parent-childres workshops
- Manufacturing educational materials
- Online conferences, digital products and learning activity books
- Presence in the French media

Dear readers,

I chose self-publishing in order to maintain all my creative freedom but I need you to make this book as visible as possible!

Some ideas to achieve this together:

- Talk about the book to education and health professionals (early childhood educator, pediatrician, psychologist, etc.), to people likely to appreciate its content.

- Leave a comment on Amazon!

- Send me a message via email at deborah@inspirationsmamans.com

Thank you in advance !

Deborah Cohen Tenoudji

Printed in Great Britain
by Amazon